Digital Transformation 3.0

The New Business-to-Consumer Connections of The Internet of Things

Chuck Martin

Books by Chuck Martin

MOBILE INFLUENCE: The New Power of the Consumer (Palgrave MacMillan)

NET FUTURE: The seven cybertrends that will drive your business, create new wealth and define your future (McGraw-Hill)

THE THIRD SCREEN: Marketing to Your Customers in a World Gone Global (Nicholas Brealey)

THE DIGITAL ESTATE: Strategies for Competing, Surviving and Thriving in an Internetworked World (McGraw-Hill)

MANAGING FOR THE SHORT TERM: The New Rules for Running a Business in a Day-to-Day World (Doubleday)

TOUGH MANAGEMENT: The 7 Ways to Make Tough Decisions Easier, Deliver the Numbers, and Grow Business in Good Times and Bad (McGraw-Hill)

MAX-e-MARKETING IN THE NET FUTURE: The Imperatives for Outsmarting the Competition in the Net Economy (co-author) (McGraw-Hill)

COFFEE AT LUNA'S: A business fable: Three Secrets to Knowledge, Self-Improvement, and Happiness in Your Work and Life (NFI Research)

Chuck Martin
Chuck@NetFutureInstitute.com

Published by NFI Research

10   9   8   7   6   5   4   3   2   1

ISBN: 978-1-98586-280-7

For further information
617-527-1363
www.digitaltransformation3.com

Cover design by Kelsey Knight
Printed in the United States of America
First Edition
Publication Date June 2018

Library of Congress Control Number: 2018903689
Library of Congress Cataloging-in Publication Data
Martin, Chuck, 1949-
     Digital Transformation 3.0: the new business-to-consumer connections of the internet of things/ chuck martin

p. cm.
Includes index.
ISBN: 978-1-98586-280-7
     1.   Internet of things. 2. Consumer behavior. 3. Internet marketing.
          4. Consumer behavior. 5. Electronic commerce. 6. Computer networks. I. Title.

To Teri

CONTENTS

Acknowledgements

In many ways, this book is a culmination of journeys through technology revolutions, the first being the Internet, the second mobile, and now, the Internet of Things. This has not been a solo journey, as I regularly run into people who have been involved in one, two, or all three innovation eras.

They are the people I want to acknowledge and thank for helping make this book a reality.

There are the countless executives involved in making the Internet of Things happen, who took time to share their stories, both the good and the bad, on their journeys. Many of them are quoted in this book and others not, so thank you to all. A special thank you to longtime colleague Doug Dreyer, Vice President Worldwide Client Centers at IBM, for arranging IoT briefings with executives during the early stages of this book research three years ago.

Thanks to those in various parts of the world who agreed to be interviewed, sometimes on short notice and sometimes at not-so-favorable times for them. Thanks to those who spoke with me for my many stories in the MediaPost AI and IoT Daily and for my global podcast "The Voices of the Internet of Things with Chuck Martin." The content and insights, both on and off the record, has been invaluable.

Mostly I want to thank my family for always indulging me, especially knowing what it takes to complete a book, having witnessed and experienced it a number of times over the years.

A big thank you to my sons Ryan and Chase, who grew up digital in our high-tech household. Thank you both, for hanging with me at high-tech events from Boston to Las Vegas CES, and for always being technologically inquisitive. I truly appreciate all your input, from helping fine-tune the title concepts to constantly bouncing IoT and new tech ideas back and forth. It means a lot to me.

And a mega-thank you to Teri, my wife and lifelong partner in everything. Especially for the reality check of every time I excitedly relay to her a brand new IoT tech innovation that's coming, and her gravity-inducing question comes: "Why would anyone want to do that?" She helps keep it all in down-to-earth context. (I also should thank our Amazon Alexa, who I sometimes catch arguing with her newest friend, Teri, and Google Home, who resides on my desk).

1 INTRODUCTION

The Third Digital Transformation

There's a technological tsunami on the horizon and it's about to shake every business to its core. This digital transformation will be bigger than any before it and will be on a global scale, transforming customer experiences along with their relationships with those they do business with. This transformation will be driven by seven major elements of the Internet of Things (IoT), comprising the interconnecting of all people, places, and things.

The first digital transformation was the Internet, or, more precisely, the commercial World Wide Web, which I documented in my 1999 bestselling book *Net Future*, which identified seven cybertrends, all of which have since come to fruition. Those were the early days of connectivity, where businesses started to digitally connect with each other, automating their supply chains, connecting employees, defining new supplier-distributor-partner relationships, and coming to grips with legacy systems.

The second digital transformation was the mobile revolution. Mobile was another game-changer, but somewhat different than the Web. With the introduction of the Internet to business, each individual had to get online, one person and one business at a time, which took a number of years. The early Web days included loading a Web browser from a disc supplied by Netscape, and later by Microsoft. No computers came with a Web browser built in at the time. When mobile hit big, starting with Apple's iPhone in 2007, everyone was already on the network. Mobile made everything portable. Rather than having to do everything online from a fixed location, sitting at a computer, the smartphone mobilized the world. Before mobile, actions were mostly serial, as in researching online at home and then leaving to go shopping, where most of the money is still spent in stores, as I documented in my 2011 *The Third Screen* and then in *Mobile Influence* in 2013.

With mobile, actions became iterative, so that people were doing things online virtually all the time and at any location. This created a wealth of new location-based information and payment services as phones evolved along with consumer behaviors.

The third transformation raining down on the world now is the Internet of Things. The major difference in this digital transformation is that rather than involving one thing, like the Internet or mobile, the Internet of Things comprises multiple things, involving rapidly evolving technology, the introduction of billions of devices becoming Internet-connected, a wealth of massive data availability, and new ways to process and analyze that data.

There are seven distinct technologically driven forces hitting the market simultaneously. The intent of this book is to put those seven forces into context, with research data and specific examples to back it up. Here are the digital transformers:

1. Sensors – These are the fuel of the Internet of Things and will facilitate tracking. In the Internet of Things, anything that moves can be tracked.

2. Artificial intelligence – Essentially the future brain of the Internet of Things, continually learning and predicting behaviors.

3. Voice assistants – The new way for people to communicate, as typing with fingers or thumbs moves to the back seat.

4. Smart homes – Internet-connected devices in the home are changing consumer expectations from the businesses they deal with.

5. Virtual, augmented reality – The merging of the physical and digital worlds, providing new real-time information and transforming locations and experiences.

6. Connected cars – Business-consumer interactions become considerably more mobile with new, all-the-time interactions.

7. Drones and robots – The automation of things people once did by remotely controlled devices that learn as they go.

There are additional technologic changes underway, such as blockchain and wearable technology, but we're highlighting the seven most relevant for businesses to start getting a handle on and dealing with today. There also is what is commonly called Industry 4.0, which refers to the fourth industrial revolution, dealing more with manufacturing and industry. This book deals more on the front end, where businesses and consumers meet and the technologies that will impact business-customer relationships.

Consumers Not Aware of IoT

One of the biggest hurdles in the adoption of Internet of Things devices by consumers is simple awareness. While many consumers have actually used or experienced IoT devices in their personal lives or at work, most are not even aware of the Internet of Things, based on a survey of 1,000 U.S. adults who have responsibility for making household financial and purchase decisions, weighted to represent the demographics of the U.S. population. It was conducted by Market Strategies. Fewer than a quarter (23 percent) of consumers are aware of the Internet of Things and the majority (68 percent) are not.

However, many have actually used or come across IoT technologies. For example, almost half have had experiences with wearable technology, including activity trackers, and about a third have had experiences with smart appliances that use Wi-Fi for remote monitoring. The study found a large difference in viewpoints between those who have familiarity with IoT and those who don't, especially related to the issue of regulations. Almost half (48 percent) of those who are familiar with the Internet of Things believe the government should regulate the use of IoT technologies in the workplace. Only a quarter of those who are not familiar with IoT say the government should regulate its use.

There are other differences based on IoT knowledge. Those who work in an IoT environment desire more IoT technologies in place -- such as smart voice -- to be used in many places throughout the day. Only half of those not in such environments have interest in any of those things.

Many consumers have heard of connected objects, like smart toothbrushes, smart refrigerators, smart cars, and smart cities. But much of the so-called smarts in many objects simply involves a device automatically being turned on or off to coincide with consumer activity. For example, the heat being turned on just before a consumer returns home, a coffee maker turned on remotely when a person awakes in the morning, or a light being turned on or off when a person enters or leaves a room are obvious examples. But the actual smarts is that the device itself gauges when it should turn on or off, based on other factors. The reality is that consumers are not likely to want IoT innovations if they don't even know about them.

The Scope of The Internet of Things

No matter how you slice it, the Internet of Things is big and some of the numbers boggle the mind. For example, 56 million smart speakers will hit the market in one year, according to a forecast from Canalys. In the smartwatch department, 80 million hybrid smartwatches will be shipping by 2022, says Juniper Research. Overall smartwatch shipments will hit 72 million units by 2021, according to IDC Research. During CES in Las Vegas, Comcast Xfinity announced it was expanding its home automation across the entire Xfinity portfolio, meaning that 15 million customers automatically and instantly got smart home capabilities at no cost. A few months later, the company rolled out a new feature to its 15 million subscribers, allowing them to instantly receive a mobile message when someone joins their network, with the ability to remotely accept or kill the connection. The location of things market is projected to reach $71 billion by 2025, according to Research and Markets. Revenue from smart audio devices will reach more than $10 billion by 2022, according to Juniper Research. One study pegs the market for IoT solutions at $1 trillion by 2022. The study by BCC Research notes that the number of Internet-connected devices already exceeds the number of people in the world. By 2022, it is projected that there will be an average of four connected devices per person globally. You get the idea.

Consumers are going to feel the impact from many aspects of the Internet of Things as more businesses move to chatbots and using artificial intelligence for dealing with customers. A quarter of customer service and support operations will include virtual customer assistant or chatbot technology within two years, according predictions from Gartner, with more than half of businesses already invested in virtual customer assistants for customer service. "As more customers engage on digital channels, VCAs are being implemented for handling customer requests on websites, mobile apps, consumer messaging apps and social networks," states Gene Alvarez, managing vice president at Gartner. "This is underpinned by improvements in natural-language processing, machine learning and intent-matching capabilities."

Gartner made additional predictions. Among them:

- By 2020, 30 percent of all B2B companies will employ artificial intelligence
- Within a year, 20 percent of brands will have abandoned their mobile apps
- More than 40 percent of all data analytics projects will relate to an aspect of customer service by 2020

- Augmented, virtual, and mixed reality immersive solutions will be adopted in 20 percent of large companies as part of their digital transformation strategy by 2020

There's a reason companies are adopting more automated technologies. After implementing virtual customer assistant technology, Gartner says businesses report a reduction of 70 percent in call, chat, or email inquiries.

Much of the information in this book is based on research from highly regarded research firms and all sources are noted where the data is used. Other information is based on my primary research, since I frequently discuss all aspects of the Internet of Things with the people in the industry who are making it happen, especially in my regular podcast "The Voices of the Internet of Things with Chuck Martin" and for my daily column in the MediaPost AI & IoT Daily, of which I am the Editor. The book is intended to be a fast read and to provide you with quick insights into varying aspects of each of the seven digital transformers to help you formulate business approaches for the future. Rather than being theoretical, the book is about what is actually happening in the market today with well-founded research on where it is heading tomorrow.

2 SENSORS

Feeling the Machines

Sensors are the fuel of the Internet of Things. They provide the real-time locations of people, places, and things. Before the commercial Web of the Internet, supply and demand could be tracked, at least in a rudimentary fashion. The Web, and especially mobile, transformed the model so that for the first time, time and location could be added to supply and demand. Those were the early days of tracking. The Internet of Things is adding an explosive new level of the tracking of everything, primarily due to the introduction and massive deployment of billions of Internet-connected devices with the power to sense all kinds of activities, providing a wealth of new data and insights. Tracking is not new, but IoT sensors can link the locations of people, places, and things in relation to each other. Often requiring very low or little power, sensors can capture and transmit bits of information. Aggregated together, many of these bits can create a vivid picture, such as a view of consumer behaviors in the context of date, time, location, distance, product inventory, pricing, and even weather at the time.

Sensors in stores can let retailers know when people come to their stores, how far they come from, where they go while in a store, how long they stay, and where they go when the leave the store. Sensors can connect with smartphones to allow messaging, such as special deals when a shopper nears certain products. Sensors in airports can aid travelers by providing relevant travel information to their phones, such as gate changes, flight delays, and boarding times. Sensors in cars can identify if a car is coming into a blind spot behind a driver, if a person or object is nearby while backing out of a garage, or if coming close to crossing a lane while driving on a highway. Sensors can be added to products consumers take home and even implanted into people, so they can unlock doors and purchase products by the simple wave of a hand.

However, all these sensors will not operate in a vacuum, since there are significant privacy issues involved, of which any major entity deploying sensors is well aware. Before capturing or using any personal information relating to sensors, consumer permission is required, so that any consumer has to actually opt in and explicitly give permission for any kind of personal tracking. The challenge for a business is to provide enough value for a consumer to want to opt in, otherwise the technology will live only in test labs. In many cases, companies are using sensors to capture aggregated information, explicitly avoiding the capture or use of any individual information. For example, a retailer may want to know shopper traffic patterns in a store to improve store layout and product placements. While store cameras have been used for this for years, sensors can make the task more efficient and accurate. Additionally, sensors can be incorporated into store lighting, which stores need anyway. This chapter intends to provide a reality check on the state of the sensors of the Internet of Things.

Sensors in Everything

Sensors are fundamental components of the Internet of Things. Coming in many forms, sensors essentially can tell when something or someone is moving and where. They can track the comings and goings of shoppers in stores, as we saw at the National Retail Federation annual show, as well as the tracking of inventory on the way to the store and as it moves around inside. Many of these sensors send information they sense over wireless networks, as might be expected in the IoT age. A pair of studies provides at least a benchmark of where the sensors market is heading.

One study, by the IoT market research firm ON World, says the majority of the sensing market will comprise Wi-Fi, Bluetooth, and private solutions, with low power wide area networks rapidly increasing. Wireless sensing, tracking, and control equipment will reach $35 billion over the next five years, according to the study. The second study, by Allied Market Research, sees the smart sensor market reaching $60 billion by 2022. Smart sensors transmit data over available networks and enable features such as digital processing and interactions with external devices. These types of sensors are found in consumer electronics, along with items in the automotive and healthcare industries. The big growth in sensors will be due to the growth in the use of them in consumer electronic devices, the development of smart cities, and the increased penetration of the Internet of Things, according to that study.

In terms of revenue generated, automotive end uses are expected to dominate for the next few years. For market share, image sensors account for the largest share, while touch sensors hold the largest share of revenue. Smart sensors will see the largest growth in North America, based on the study.

For brands and marketers, this means more customer tracking will be possible with more precise and a larger amount of location information available. And that is one of the most significant marketing uses of sensors coming. Consumers will start to find themselves finding sensors and other tracking devices in many of the regular places they visit.

Sensors Everywhere

Cameras everywhere. That's one of the promises of the Amazon Go store that opened to the public after more than a year of testing with Amazon employees. Shoppers use their phones to identify themselves as they enter the store, pick up items as they shop, and when done, walk out the door, triggering a charge of all the groceries to their Amazon account. This is well beyond the established practice of self-scanning and self-checkout and is accomplished through tracking. Make that *lots* of tracking. Amazon says it uses "computer vision, deep learning algorithms, sensor fusion, much like you'd find in self-driving cars."

Cameras have been used in stores for many years, such as in big box retailers to measure traffic patterns. In recent years, tracking has gotten much better, thanks to the introduction of IoT sensors, such as beacons. Dwell time, the amount of time a person spends in a store, has been one of the benefits to marketers, as well as knowing how many customers are repeat customers and what likely drove them back to the store.

At the annual Big Show put on by the National Retail Federation, various forms of in-store camera usage were highlighted. The key is that in-store cameras can be used for different things. For example, AT&T and Samsung displayed cameras that tracked customers in the aggregate, creating heat maps of traffic patterns. Meanwhile, NEC showed cameras used for identifying specific customers and tracking them as they travel the store aisles, providing targeted messaging to them on screen displays in the store. Many in-store display screens have cameras built in, so in addition to providing messaging to shoppers, they also can capture demographics of who is actually seeing those messages.

Cameras in screens in stores are not new, but the tracking technology involved is getting significantly better. Targeted messaging via facial recognition is a major marketing goal here. The question is how much consumers will realize about this technology and, of those who do, what their reaction might be. If nothing else, Amazon Go may provide a glimpse of consumer reaction. Especially, as shoppers come to realize that everything they do when in a store is monitored. Closely.

Facial recognition continues to improve greatly, and one system using deep learning technology was introduced by Panasonic. The high-precision face recognition software can identify faces including at an angle, those partially hidden by sunglasses, and those that are difficult to recognize with conventional technologies, according to Panasonic. The software features the iA (intelligent auto) mode, which automatically adjusts to shoot optimal images for face recognition and the best shots are then sent to the server for recognition. With conventional facial recognition systems, all the images are sent to the server, where the recognition occurs.

"Using this software with cameras equipped with the iA function enables image analysis to be performed on the camera instead of the server to send only the best images to the server," states the announcement by Panasonic. "This will result in reducing server and network loads, which leads to overall system cost reductions. In the case of 10 or more network cameras are connected to the system, the costs can be reduced by about 40 percent to 50 percent compared to conventional systems that do not use the Best Shot function."

Panasonic plans to add a function to recognize faces partially covered, such as by a surgical mask. The system, which will be launched in July, can include an expansion kit enabling it to register up to 30,000 faces. Panasonic suggests the system could be used at airports or train stations to help prevent acts of terror. Sensors of all types also can provide businesses with many different customer insights, though it may sound easier than it actually is to accomplish.

Wearables Sales Growth

Wearable sales will grow an average of 20 percent each year over the next five years, according to a one forecast, with worldwide wearable sales reaching $29 billion with 243 million devices shipping by 2022, based on the forecast by CCS Insight. Apple is set to pass worldwide sales of Swiss-made watches annually. In China, 25 million connected watches for children were sold in a one-year period. Over the next five years, 30 million hearable devices are expected to be sold.

Desired uses of wearable devices are also getting more specific, with companies tapping artificial intelligence to give consumers actionable information for fitness wearables, according to a fitness wearables study. Fitness devices also are expanding, with strong growth in clothing and ear-based fitness wearables projected. The shipment of such devices will grow 60 percent a year over the next four years, according to the report by Juniper Research.

This means specialized wearable devices will account for 25 percent of the market within a few years.

Wearables began with fitness trackers and then branched out into more sophisticated devices, most notably the Apple

Watch, though not in the category of fitness trackers. Fitness trackers basically became *smarter* over time, providing health measures, such as steps taken, heart rate, and oxygenation. The ongoing challenge for fitness trackers is continued usage. For example, fewer than 60 percent of registered users of Fitbit devices are classed as active users in any given year, according to the study.

Going forward, there are three elements a fitness wearable must have to succeed, according to Juniper Research.

- Multiple metrics – Tracking numerous metrics, such as heart rate, calorie burn, distance, location and step counting, will be required and made possible by the miniaturization of a range of sensors that can feed more information into a system.

- Artificial intelligence – Some companies are promoting their products as having AI, leading to the analytics platform being the primary offering of wearables. The data platform is projected to become more important to consumers than the device.

- Targeted fitness – Several wearables now target more precise uses, such as smart running shoes, biometric-tracking hearables and specialist running smartwatches. These types of devices are not intended to be constantly worn and are likely to be higher priced.

One of the most significant expectations from AI being used in wearables is the addition of voice-based advice on training techniques, according to Juniper. This advice is expected to be delivered via hearables. Voice is entering yet another area of the Internet of Things, as detailed in a later chapter.

The Hybrid Smartwatch

The smartwatch market is getting a bit more complicated. Since the Apple Watch launched in 2014, the common perception of smartwatches was that they could do a lot more than just tell time. Juniper Research defines a smartwatch as a wrist-based wearable that emulates traditional watch designs, as well as providing additional digital functionality.

However, the research firm divides smartwatches into two categories. The first category comprises display smartwatches that have a digital display and may run an on-device operating system, such as Apple Watch or Android Wear. The second category involves hybrid watches, which have analogue faces and provide limited connected functions, such as step tracking or notifications. Examples of hybrid watches are Fossil Q Hybrid watches, MyKronoz ZeWatch and Withings Activite. The way the market is shaping up is that there is no one main driver of the watches. For example, the most important smartwatch applications are all over the map, such as fitness (34 percent), communication (30 percent), maps (28 percent), health (28 percent) and social media (16 percent), according to the Juniper report.

Emerging out of all of this is the hybrid smartwatch. The new forecast has 80 million hybrid smartwatches shipping by 2022. IDC forecasts put smartwatch shipments at 72 million units overall by 2021.No matter, it is a large number. The key is that there will be a pretty even split between hybrid and display smartwatches with the hybrids longer battery life appealing to a larger audience than display smartwatches, according to the forecast. The hot smartwatches of the future just won't necessarily have to be as *smart* as smartwatches have been perceived for some time. Future owners of hybrid smartwatches essentially will be able to wear a timepiece with a foot in the past and a foot in the future.

Backing Out of Wearables

The wearables device market also can be tough. While research shows that interest around wearable devices focused on health and fitness, at least in terms of what kinds of information consumers want from their devices, those devices won't be coming from Adidas. The company somewhat backed out of wearables, shuttering its Digital Sports business unit, the group that develops the company's wearables tech. "To further drive our digital transformation and win the consumer in this dynamic business environment, we have redefined our strategic approach towards digital, sharpening our focus on digital experiences," an Adidas spokesperson told me. "In this context, we decided to discontinue running a stand-alone digital sports organization. Instead we are integrating digital across all areas of our business and will continue to grow our digital expertise, but in a more integrated way."

This essentially means that Adidas is going to spread its wearables activities into other areas of the company and stop making wearable devices themselves. "One example of how we are planning to sharpen our focus on digital experiences is consolidating the adidas app eco-system and discontinue All Day," says the spokesperson. "We will focus our efforts on two powerful brand platforms, Runtastic and the adidas App in an effort to create the best digital experience for our consumer." Adidas does have a deal with Fitbit, so the idea of Adidas totally walking away from wearables is not happening.

Meanwhile, Nokia announced it was conducting a "review of strategic options" for its wearables business, which is part of Nokia Technologies. The company has been selling hybrid smartwatches, scales, and other digital health devices. Nokia says the review may result in a "transaction or other changes."

When they first came out, wearables -- especially fitness trackers -- were a relatively big hit, since they could provide easy monitoring of various activities, such as steps taken, heart rate, and floors climbed. By now, almost half (48 percent) of U.S. adults have experienced at least some wearable technology, according to a survey by Market Strategies. Wearables makers can't stand still, as various features expand into other devices like smartwatches. In a bid for continued relevance, wearables band market pioneer Fitbit acquired Twine Health, a health coaching platform that helps people manage chronic conditions.

One major issue is continued usage. Fewer than 60 percent of registered Fitbit devices are classed as active users in any given year, according to Juniper Research. The types of wearables are also increasing, most notably in clothing and ear-based fitness devices. Sensors are becoming smaller and better, enabling more of them to be embedded in more places and increasing monitoring capabilities. Whether worn on wrists or elsewhere, more wearable technology will be ending up on more consumers. How long they keep them on is still the market metric to be determined.

While some areas of wearables transition, they are booming in China. Fitbit fitness trackers were not initially a hit in China, but the subsequent arrival of less expensive trackers, such as the Mi Band, drove mass adoption by consumers. The launch of the Apple Watch in 2015 also was popular for a rising middle class. By 2021, eMarketer estimates that nearly a quarter of adult internet users in China will regularly use a wearable. "Wearable devices will continue to experience high growth among consumers in China," says Shelleen Shum, senior forecasting analyst at eMarketer. "Thanks to the availability of inexpensive devices with constantly improving functionalities, coupled with an enthusiasm for new technology among working adults, the adoption of wearable technology is on the rise."

What People Want from Wearables

First there was the novelty of seeing how many steps or miles you have walked, jogged, or run or how many flights of stairs climbed in a day. Then it became a competitive sport, so consumers could see where they fit in relation to peers, colleagues or friends. Wearables entered the mobile payment arena, so the tap of a wearable at checkout could trigger a payment. Wrist devices also could provide haptic feedback as a reminder of something to do or even provide hands-free directions. Of all the potential uses for wearable devices, the leading categories relating to what types of information consumers want relates to health, according to a study from Forrester. The study comprised a survey of 33,000 U.S. online adults. Here are the types of information consumers would want from a wearable device, according to the study:

- 30% -- Health and fitness
- 20% -- Notifications and communication
- 20% -- Travel, such as hands-free directions
- 15% -- Retail recommendations, such as local deals
- 12% -- Monitoring activities, such as babies

A quarter (25 percent) of online consumers already own a wearable device and 17 percent of those use them for health and fitness, according to Forrester. The number of people with wearables is projected to grow to 28 percent over the next five years, with millennials leading the way. However, the market is changing. Rather than wearable such as fitness trackers dominating in the future, it will be the smartwatch. By 2022, it will be more than 50 percent, with well over 44 million total wearables being sold, according to Forrester. This is consistent with other studies. The other IoT dynamic is that more wearables are becoming standalone, with their own network connectivity, making a smartphone less of a requirement. The categories and type of wearables will continue to evolve over time. Meanwhile, the total number will just keep rising.

Wearables for Payments

The capabilities of wearables continue to evolve, but there's one feature that may give a real boost to adoption of the devices, and that's the ability to pay for something. That feature is the ability to pay for something via a wearable device, such as a smartwatch or fitness tracker. The majority (60 percent) of consumers say they would be interested in using a contactless form of payment, like by a smartwatch, to pay for something while exercising, according to one study. For millennials, it's even higher, with 80 percent interested in using a wearable device for paying while exercising. For baby boomers, that number is 38 percent.

The study comprised a survey of 1,000 adults in a representative sample of the U.S. population conducted by Wakefield Research for Visa. Almost half (49 percent) of consumers say they have wanted to make a purchase immediately before or after exercising but could not because they didn't have a form of payment with them. Even more (70 percent) millennials felt the same way. More than half (57 percent) of consumers say they have put a form of payment somewhere while exercising. Here's where consumers put their form of payment while they exercise or work out:

- 56% -- In a pocket

- 32% -- In a sock or shoe
- 24% -- Inside the waistband of pants or shorts
- 24% -- In undergarments, such as underwear or bra
- 18% -- Held it in their hand the entire time
- 8% -- Put in in a hat

A third (33 percent) of millennials put their payment method in their undergarments, compared to 14 percent of baby boomers. Most Americans (71 percent) carry some form of payment with them while exercising or working out but fewer than a third (28 percent) have it in a smartphone or wearable device. That's an opportunity for smartwatches and fitness trackers, since many of those exercising or working out already have that device literally on them.

Leveraging Location Data

Identifying where a consumer is at any given moment and creating relevant messaging delivered in context has been a marketing goal since forever. Beacons started to help a little in stores over the last few years and, along with Wi-Fi location and the old GPS standby, knowing where a person is located has somewhat improved. Companies like InMarket and Philips Lighting have figured ways to link the location of shoppers with specific products near them in stores, creating proper incentives to drive the sales of some of those products. InMarket taps beacons while Philips uses connected lights. The promise of Internet-connected technologies is that the billions of sensors that will be deployed will continually supply a wealth of much more precise consumer location data. However, that is *then* and this is now.

At the moment, advertisers are challenged in working with location data due to the varied levels of mobile marketing maturity combined with the complexity associated with the large number of sources and technologies that comprise the location landscape, according to a study comprising a survey of 200 marketing decision makers in organizations that spend $250 million or more annually on advertising in North America. It was conducted by Forrester Consulting for Verve. Many organization are challenged in using location date, for a host of reasons.

Challenges using location data (Forrester)

- 34% -- Inaccurate location data
- 33% -- Understanding how to use location to deliver relevant messaging
- 30% -- Lack of clarity on what third-party vendors or providers exist
- 29% -- Perception within the company that existing social media marketing efforts overlap
- 28% -- Difficulty defining the targeting to apply
- 28% -- Difficulty combining mobile location with other customer data
- 27% -- Lack of transparency in location data collection
- 27% -- Difficulty passing exposure data back into a data management platform
- 27% -- Achieving scale of reach
- 25% -- Lack of clarity on the sources of location data

The Internet of Things won't cure all of this, but it will help identify where a consumer is located. Even with sophisticated location-tracking technology, when it really matters, some find their way back to traditional basics.

Trusting Location Tracking

The Internet of Things involves the blending of a lot of new and a lot of old. Over one summer weekend, many tall ships sailed into Boston Harbor at an event called Sail Boston, part of the Rendez-Vous 2017 Tall Ships Regatta, a transatlantic race celebrating the 150th anniversary of the Canadian Confederation. The Regatta covers 7,000 nautical miles and visits six countries, with Boston being the only stop in the U.S. The oldest of the 55 ships was built in 1893 and the newest in 2016. I spent some time on two of the most significant ships, the 295-foot U.S. Coast Guard Eagle and the 379-foot Tall Ship Union from Peru, the largest ship in the fleet, to check out some of the old and the new.

In true IoT fashion, the Union, built in 2015 and carrying a crew of 250, has all the latest gadgetry in its high-tech bridge. There are sensors throughout the ship that show on a large screen the current status of energy generation and usage, water on board, and the status of each system, whether running or not. This is in addition to digital displays of charts, speeds, depths, and various other measurements along with keyboards and multiple communications systems. The ship is clearly designed to tap the latest connected technologies for operations, navigations, and many other functions. However, on a very large table in the same pilothouse was a large paper chart, on which manual chart plotting tools, including a parallel ruler and a pencil, about as old school as you can get. The ship officer showing me the technology says they do not totally rely on the technology, but rather the actual paper course plotting. I asked why, with all the state-of-the-art technological capabilities provided, they would rely on a paper-plotted course rather than the technology. "We don't totally trust it," he says.

I found a somewhat similar situation on the U.S. Coast Guard Eagle, which was built in 1936 and is used as a training ship for cadets. Rather than digital sensors like the Union, the Eagle uses video cameras to track every important function in the ship. There's a screen in the wheelhouse showing all the camera angles as well as a large TV-sized screen showing all the camera feeds in the officers' meeting room below deck. The ship also has all the digital technology needed to navigate. However, as part of the training while at sea, all the technology is turned off at times so the cadets learn how to navigate and run the ship without any technology, Coast Guard Lt. Eric Johnson told me during my ship tech tour. The cadets learn the technology but are trained to work without it.

Meanwhile, shipbuilders in Japan are working to develop an artificial-intelligence-driven steering system that, using various IoT technologies, would simultaneously gather and analyze data about weather while at sea, shipping information, and dangerous obstacles, according to a report in Nikkei Asian Review. The smart ships would use AI to predict malfunctions and plot the most fuel-efficient and safest routes. The plan is to build more than 200 self-navigating systems, and the end goal is to implement fully unmanned shipping sometime in the future. In a tragic irony, a Japanese cargo ship and U.S. Navy destroyer collided just outside of Tokyo Bay, with a defense expert telling The Daily Mail that he believed the container ship was on autopilot, which many ships use while at sea.

AI and IoT technology is being tapped in every industry, from shipping to retail, automotive, travel, and hospitality. However, as the technology rapidly advances, human factors and human interactions still have a major role. If a sensor on the Union ship detects a problem, someone has to actually deal with it. For the cameras to be effective on the Eagle, someone has to be monitoring the video feeds. Automation, thanks to

24

connected things, is growing. So is the need for people monitoring those connected and automated things.

ID on Location

New security methods around connected things may help consumers more safely pay for things they are buying. Biometric identifiers are growing and providing new ways to authenticate who someone is. One method of identification is a fingerprint scan. In 2013, only two smartphone models had fingerprint sensors on them, but now, more than 200 different models have them, according to Juniper Research.

There also is a process called two-factor authorization. That's when a consumer has a physical thing, like a credit card, and then something else, like a password or PIN. A second factor also could be a text message. Starting with the Galaxy S8, Samsung has yet another identification form, via its eye scanner. A nearby beacon also could validate that a particular phone is in a certain location.

Many of these innovations are aimed at making transactions more secure. Mobile biometric payment volumes are around two billion, says Juniper. And then there's voice. More than a million banking customers of Citi in the Asia Pacific region have used the company's voice biometrics authentication service, in the course of less than a year, according to Citi. The Internet of Things involves lots of automating of processes and payments are a large target. More advanced methods involve putting microchips into people, as companies in Sweden and Belgium have been doing. In those cases, a wave of a hand can trigger a payment or unlock a door. Implanting chips in people has occurred in the United States as well. More than in people, connected and transmitting devices will find their way into countless of everyday locations where consumers regularly pass by, including on and in shelves at stores.

Shopping Shelf Sensors

Among many other connected or smart devices at the National Retail Federation Big Show in New York was the smart shelf. Smart shelves are hardly a new concept and have been around for years, but developments in sensors and connectivity are now making them more practical. I saw displays of smart shelves from various companies at the trade show. One of the more interesting, from Powershelf, is even marketed as a service through a partnership with Hitachi. In that case, the retailer would get the shelves along with all the associated capabilities without an actual purchase of the shelves. The shelves, essentially an entirely networked device, provide for electronic price tags placed in front of the items just behind it on the shelf, much like printed price tags typically found in most stores.

The key is the connectivity. When an item is lifted off the shelf, it automatically triggers the inventory system to notify it that an item is at least being considered. When a shelf is empty, the system triggers a restocking alert to store personnel, John Wright, CEO of Powershelf, told me at the show. If inventory of a product is high, a specific inventory-based offer could occur in real time, such as when a shopper picks up an item, the pricing message could offer 'two for the price of one.' Pricing is dynamic and can be based on inventory, essentially more effectively matching supply and demand. The shelf I saw also contained a beacon so that a smartphone message could be triggered to a shopper near the shelf. The Internet of Things is going to totally transform shopping, involving all aspects of retail.

In Retail

Retailers are gradually moving to smart shelves, which include small displays for dynamic pricing along with sensors that can tell when a product is taken off the shelf by a customer. Some shelving also hosts a beacon, to trigger communications to a nearby shopper who has opted in. However, the shelves are but one connected location and would typically be found in a grocery store, which contains many products. What became clear as I wandered through the halls and aisles of the National Retail Federation's annual Big Show in New York, was that all kinds of connections are going to be coming to a large number of stores. Many pieces of clothing already are coming with tags to be tracked. At the NRF show, there were many and all kinds of sensing tags, such as those prominently hanging from dresses and other apparel on hangers. There were sensors in LED lighting, such as those from Philips Lighting, which can pinpoint a shopper in a store in the context of all the products around them.

Samsung showed a sensor that peers down at clothing or other items from above and tracks the movement of those products, providing a heat map of product movement over time. Pepper the Robot from Softbank included sensors that can tell if a person is smiling or not, along with some of their likely demographic traits. There were sensors, now costing pennies rather than dollars, on products that could be automatically read at checkout and, if desired, by paid by smartwatch or smartphone. Cisco showed what, in effect, was a set of sensors from above, using a small antenna to create a beaconing effect on the floor, in real time, without requiring physical beacons in any locations. The interesting twist at NRF is that much of the novelty of smart and connected things seems to have worn off a bit. This is a good thing, since demonstrations and discussions are now less about the cool new technology and more about the benefits and results promised to be delivered by those innovations. Eventually, sensors will be in clothing for various reasons, but not until the consumers marketplace is ready for it.

Almost in Clothing

Tracking consumers through sensors inside clothing they buy from L.L. Bean now will not be happening. It was reported in numerous publications around the world that Bean would be starting a clothes tracking test with customers later this year. Bean now says that is not going to happen. "I can absolutely confirm that L.L. Bean will not be selling clothes with this technology to consumers," Shawn Gorman, chairman of L.L. Bean, told me. "We may test some items with product testers who consent to this, but not to normal customers. Loomia, which makes a blockchain-powered smart fabric, had previously announced a partnership with L.L. Bean to bring its blockchain fabric knowledge to the Maine retailer. The smart fabric technology can capture information such as temperature, how commonly a particular item of clothing is worn and how moisture is acquired. It was earlier reported that Bean was planning to sew such sensors into boots and coats and then track the clothes after they leave the store through the Ethereum blockchain. The sensors likely could also track steps taken and other data.

The tracking was to start later this year and be opt in, according to the many reports, quoting a Bean innovation employee. "The reports that have been in the media circulating suggesting that L.L. Bean is going to be selling products embedded with sensors that track our customers' habits is 100 percent false," a Bean spokesperson told me. "We are not, have not, nor do we ever intend to sell any product that tracks anyone's buying habits, physical movements or collects any form of demographic information. "This was a concept only, aimed to provide testing information for product performance," says the spokesperson. "The field testing would have been done by a very small cohort of volunteers, not customers. In additionally, this is not testing we will be pursuing."

Clothing with embedded sensors has been around for some time. At the National Federation of Retailers Big Show, Levi Strauss showed RFID tags in jeans, allowing retailers to track the real-time status of inventory. The tracking was also aimed at clothing being taken into dressing rooms. That technology was intended for in-store use only. L.L. Bean is also dealing with customer reaction to its announcement of scrapping its age-old 'guaranteed for life policy' of products it sells, now giving customers one year to return items as long as they have a receipt.

The IoT reality is that sensors are going to find their way into anything that moves, including clothing and even packaged goods. The technology will be ready for this before the market is -- the Bean clothes idea may be a good example of this. "I think the story just got a little ahead of itself," says the Bean spokesperson. "We look at lots of technologies in the marketplace. It's a difference of concept vs. actively pursuing." For now, it looks like the tracking of clothes that consumers buy may remain in the concept category, at least in the case of L.L. Bean. The technology is being developed at times well ahead of the market's ability to absorb it.

Store Sensors

Smart technology to get shoppers out of stores more quickly is coming. However, it's coming less like a freight train and more like a glacier. Smart checkout can comprise different techniques, such as totally checkout-less shopping, cashier-based automatic payment and automatic item scanning and bagging, according to a new study by Juniper Research. The capabilities are enabled by a variety of sensor and image recognition technologies, though most are in the trial stages. The general idea is that shoppers come into a store, browse and select products and, when done, can leave more quickly while bypassing checkout lines. Anyone who has made a purchase in an Apple store can see one approach, with customers paying an in-aisle salesperson and even the associate who helped them select a product. Amazon Go takes this to another level, with shoppers putting items in bags and technology tracking the process so a person leaves the store and then is charged.

More than $78 billion in transactions will be processed through smart checkouts within five years, according to Juniper. The number of stores involved is large, projected to be in more than 5,000 retail outlets in five years. The number of consumers using checkout apps, allowing them to scan their own items, will grow from to 30 million in five years, according to the forecast.

Retailers will have some incentive to deploy such systems, with Juniper estimating that the new *invisible payment* checkout technologies will drive an average increase in revenue of more than $300 per shopper by 2022. These include checkout apps and automatic scanning, pretty basic functions relative to more comprehensive IoT approaches. However, the cost to deploy totally smart checkouts will be slow due to the high cost of the technology with pressure to show ROI. Meanwhile, consumers can continue to do their shopping online or in a store and then, to skip a line, simply order online for either delivery or in-store pickup. That can get them out of a store quickly. Sensors also are going to cause changes for how retailers adapt to in-store shopper behavior.

Connecting Retail Customers

Retailers will connect to IoT platforms more than 12 billion *things*, including digital signs, products and, most notably, Bluetooth beacons, by 2021, according to one forecast. This would be an increase of 350 percent from earlier years, according to Juniper Research, which segments the IoT opportunities for retailers into three arenas:

- Customer behavior. The role of the Internet of Things is to understand the consumer on an individual level, where previously assumptions have been made on a macro level. The idea is that this will create much-improved customer relationships and sales conversions.

- Customer experience. The aim of this segment is to insure that the consumer's experience is satisfactory to the point that the shopper will return to the store based on prior shopping experiences. This will be driven by emerging and immature technologies playing a key role.

- Supply chain. The least relevant to marketers, but greater insights into the supply chain and more real-time information will be required to fuel the first two.

In the key segment of customer behavior, Bluetooth beacons are seen as one of the most significant developments, especially because of the latest major entry, the Google Eddystone beacon format. That standard allows for beacon communication with Physical Web supported browsers, eliminating the need to have a specific app on a phone to receive beacon-triggered messaging. The standard already has gained some traction in the marketplace. Boston-based Swirl, one of the earliest and largest ad platform companies to tap into beacons, introduced its integration with Google's beacon registry. This created an automated way to deploy and manage large-scale proximity marketing programs. A drag on beacon programs has been the requirements for a consumer to have a specific app on their smartphone and having Bluetooth turned on when in range of a beacon. In addition, most beacon programs were pretty much closed networks, lacking any large industry standard. Google changes that with its new standards, with the massive Google beacon platform now connected via the Swirl marketing platform.

The Swirl integration allows non-technical people at retailers and brands to manage their location signals and in-store shopper experiences. The beacon deployments are part of the many billions of connected devices coming. Such technologies can contribute to new shopping experiences. IoT technologies are going to significantly impact retail. Connected shelves I saw at the National Retail Federation Big Show can track inventory, dynamically change prices, and, with beacons included, link shoppers with products. This is being done at a Carrefour hypermarket in France with connected lights by Philips Lighting. Studies consistently show that consumers make most purchases in physical stores. Thanks to the Internet of Things, much more interaction with those in-store shoppers is just around the corner. Sensors like beacons in stores can also present an opportunity to improve marketing messages to consumers.

Beacons for Advertising

The idea of marketers targeting consumers based on their location is hardly new. However, the location information has been improving greatly over time, thanks in part to data from various sensors, most notably beacons. Ad campaigns have been created based on location patterns, such as how long a person stays in a particular store or fast food restaurant and where they come from and where they go from there. When it was owned by Qualcomm, beacon-maker Gimbal specialized in large venues, such as sporting arenas. Gimbal later was acquired by The Mobile Majority, a Los Angeles-based mobile advertising firm and the two were integrated, says Gimbal CEO Rob Emrich, who gave me a rundown after the Gimbal acquisition. The big thing for Gimbal is attribution, linking advertising with where a person goes and how long they stay there. The concept is to measure whether a certain customer drove by a store or stopped and went in, and if they did, where did they go and how long did they stay, says Emrich.

"Location is becoming more and more important, allowing advertisers to create micro-targeting campaigns," Emrich says. "Beacons are a way to be more precise." Gimbal uses GPS tracking by geofencing locations along with its beacons, which are linked to apps in more than 35 million mobile devices, Emrich says. "We do targeting and attribution. Customers are asking for attribution and they want to know how well their media is using location. They want to know, 'did someone take an action after seeing this ad?'" The Mobile Majority already had a media buying platform and Gimbal had a location services infrastructure. The merger of the two essentially created a data and software company, one that focuses on location-based media buying. Beacons are hardly the end game relating to location tracking in the Internet of Things. Ultimately, anyone or anything that moves will be trackable. The true value may ultimately be in the aggregate of all that data, which can be captured from anywhere beacons are located, even at airports.

London Airport Beacons

Beacons at retail have been chugging along in various tests and trials, with some large deployments. The promise of beacons in that context has been the ability to deliver more relevant messaging based on location or to gather information-based location insights for later or other uses, as previously discussed. However, when used as a service, beacons can be used to help people get around. That's just what the U.K.'s Gatwick Airport. did, by installing 2,000 beacons across its two terminals to enable a reliable 'blue dot' on indoor maps. As an added IoT twist, Gatwick added an augmented reality wayfinding tool, so passengers could be shown directions in the camera view of their smartphone. Airport execs say Gatwick is not collecting any personal data, though generic information on people densities in different beacon zone may be used to improve airport operations, such as queue management and reducing congestion.

For marketing, retailers and other third parties may also use the beacon system to detect proximity and send relevant offers or promotional messages to passengers who opt to receive them. "We are proud to be the first airport to deploy augmented reality technology and we hope that our adoption of this facility influences other airports and transport providers so that it eventually becomes the norm," says Abhi Chacko, head of IT commercial and innovation, Gatwick Airport. Gatwick also is in discussions with airlines to enable the beacon-triggered wayfinding tool into their apps. While the beacons can't make airlines depart or arrive on time, at least they can help travelers find their way around the airport while they wait. Sensors of all types are being deployed at any place where consumer go.

Connected Coolers

The Internet of Things will impact retail in countless ways and some of them are starting to be seen. There are smart dressing rooms, in-aisle automatic payments, beacons, and all types of customer tracking technologies, such as connected lights that can pinpoint a smartphone location to within inches, as we've discussed. Some of the leaders of companies behind such innovations presented their strategies at a conference that dealt with all sides of the Internet of Things. The usual industrial-focused applications, such as what GE is doing with jet engines, were discussed, along with some that were much more consumer-facing.

One of the most interesting discussions at the Connected Things conference held by the MIT Enterprise Forum of Cambridge held at the MIT Media Lab focused on retail. During a panel discussion 'Connected Retail: Running the Store with IoT,' Jumbi Edulbehram, regional president, Americas, of Oncam, showed how the company's 360-degree technology is used in stores so that multiple users can simultaneously look at different parts of the image, which captures video of very large parts of a store from one device. The camera can be used for tracking, analyzing how long lines are, heat mapping, and counting people in different parts of a store. Another technology for in-store tracking was shown by Kaynam Hedayat, vice president of product management and marketing at Digital Lumens. The connected lighting can track store assets as well as lead shoppers to what they are looking for.

One of the most interesting involved video displays now installed in 2,500 Budweiser beer cooler doors. The displays include multiple IoT sensors, so they can measure temperature, door opening or closing, and product proximity, Sanjay

Manandhar, founder and president of Aerva, tells me. He says the door also can control dynamic pricing, since the messaging is all centrally controlled by Anheuser-Busch in St. Louis. Aerva, founded more than 10 years ago by MIT alum, essentially provides the IoT platform for the data collection and screen messaging. Rather than the traditional clear door of beer coolers, the Budweiser doors become screens that display branded videos, graphics, and animations customized for each region. Anheuser-Busch effectively created its own digital cooler network, giving it control of in-store experiences of shoppers near the coolers. These types of IoT innovations are popping up all over the retail landscape, setting the stage for new customer interactions.

Other beverage coolers also are getting connected. Around a million Red Bull branded beverage coolers around the world are being connected by AT&T. The goal of the connected coolers is to provide data relating to performance, temperature stats and geolocation information, according to AT&T. From a marketing perspective, the data also will provide shopper frequency insight from door activity from coolers around the world. Each time a door is opened or closed, an embedded monitor notes the data and sends it to the AT&T Control Center, which processes the data from each cooler.

This isn't the first connected cooler implementation. There are 2,500 Budweiser beer cooler doors fitted with multiple IoT sensors, so they can measure temperature, door opening or closing and product proximity. In the Budweiser connected coolers, the doors become screens that display branded videos, graphics and animations customized for each reason, Sanjay Manandhar, founder of Aerva, the company that does the connecting, told me. In both cases, the justification can be the tracking of inventory or the status of each unit, to help identify issues early. The side benefits for marketers may be even more significant, as consumer behaviors can be monitored in relation to specific products, by location, in real time, one of the major promises of the Internet of Things. Sensors also can be incorporated into product packaging.

Connected Tostitos

While the Internet of Things will give birth to billions of sensors designed and deployed for the long term, one-shot or temporary connectivity approaches are starting to bloom. Connected bracelets, or as Disney calls them, *MagicBands*, allow Disney World visitors to enter the parks, unlock hotel room doors, and buy food and merchandise. Wristbands with barcodes can be quickly printed at the Museum of Science in Boston, allowing visitors to do an instant scan and get a detailed computer analysis of their walking characteristics or check in at the facial recognition station to see what animals cause their pupils to change size. After leaving the museum, visitors can enter their wristband ID online to review their museum activities.

Temporary connectivity now is being taken to another level, targeted explicitly to Super Bowl Sunday party-goers. Special bags of Tostitos tortilla chips were outfitted with NFC chips featuring an alcohol sensor near the Tostitos logo on the front of the bag. The 'party safe' bag, created by Goodby Silverstein and Partners, provided a reminder not to drive after drinking by lighting up on the front of the bag a red steering wheel with the message 'Don't drink and drive.' The bag incorporated smart LED lights to generate colors that help illustrate the user experience.

"Our bag comes equipped with a sensor for alcohol detection, a custom manufactured PCB, which is a micro controller, and intelligent LEDs," says Roger Baran, creative director at Goodby Silverstein and Partners. "The system is calibrated to detect even the smallest traces of alcohol on a person's breath. The PCB is integrated with the smart LEDs to generate the three colors that make the user experience: blue for standby, red when alcohol is detected and green when no alcohol is detected. The entire system, including sensor, PCB, the ring of LEDs and the batteries, is integrated into the bag, which was printed and assembled in a special process." At the top center of the limited-edition bags is a small circle with the message 'blow here.' "The instructions on the back of the bag direct people to wait for a full blue circle to appear and blow hard two inches away from the bag, and directly at the sensor on the where they can read 'blow here,' says Sam Luchini, creative director at GSP.

Tostitos partnered with Mothers Against Drunk Driving (MADD) to offer 25,000 party-goers $10 off an Uber ride on Super Bowl Sunday. All they had to do was scan the barcode on the bag, get the code and enter it into their Uber app. Those with an Android phone only needed to tap their phone to the bag to initiate the Uber app. At the very least, the connected bag could be a great conversation piece on Super Bowl Sunday. At best, it could remove from the road the first 25,000 potential drivers who see the Tostitos lights turn red. Sensors are getting so small and sophisticated they can almost go anywhere, even inside medicine.

The Networked Pill

The networked pill is here. The FDA has approved the first U.S. drug with a digital ingestion tracking system. The digital pill, called Abilify MyCite, has a sensor inside that records that the medication was taken. The pill doesn't really work alone; it sends a message from its sensor to a wearable patch, which then transmits the info to a mobile app. The idea is that patients can track the ingestion of the medication on their smartphone. This particular trackable pill is used to treat schizophrenia.

Trackable medication has been in the works for many years. In 2008, MIT Technology Review documented a Silicon Valley startup that developed a system that identified pill taking by using sensors that monitored the body's responses. Of course, there are potential unintended consequences and countless potential minefields around trackable pills. For example, doctors or insurance companies could track whether certain medications were taken and incent or penalize certain behaviors. In one type of system, a pill's signal is sent electrically via skin tissues and could be detected remotely by a company wanting to check what medications potential employees are taking, as noted in the 2008 MIT story.

Opt in Becomes Contract in

There are an almost infinite number of sensor possibilities to deal with, depending on the type of business. For example, retail will be impacted, since so many customers come and go in and out of stores, as well as meander around departments inside. Same for quick serve restaurants, with plenty of repeat customers. Appliance repair is another key place for sensors, as noted earlier in this chapter. One thing to remember is that sensors can be used to track pretty much anything and anyone. However, just because something or someone *can* be tracked doesn't necessarily mean it *should* be tracked. And that is of paramount importance.

All tracking of individuals has to be opt in, as every marketer is keenly aware. However, many opt in executions are buried within the fine print or in countless lines of text that many consumers don't read. That may have worked in the early days of the Net and the early days of mobile, but the Internet of Things is different.

For this third digital transformation, the opt in of the past two digital transformations is going to be replaced by what I call the *contract in*. With contract in, consumers are going to have to be convinced that the value proposition is strong enough for the consumer to agree to be interacted with, at the right time, and in the right way. This means pre-selling a consumer on future benefits and gearing to be able to anticipate consumer needs in advance. This is way beyond getting a consumer to agree to receive text message offers or advance word of sales. Contract in will be personal and businesses will have to earn it. Companies will need to determine value propositions well in advance and essentially attempt to convince willing customers. Overall, this transformation means fewer, but better, customers. Sensors will drive the entire rethinking of customer acquisition, since the mass deployment of sensors changes the potential interactions and engagements with consumers.

Sensors will allow the tracking of people and things in relation to each other and in advance.

For example, sensors in lights can signal phones at Carrefour in France to identify precise locations of shoppers, while product inventory could be tracked by sensors, thereby matching the two. Amazon is doing similar things with camera technology in Amazon Go stores. You saw other examples earlier in this chapter.

Sensors are not about the technology. This is about the new capabilities being created that will provide new ways to engage with customers based on where they are, where they have been, and where they are likely going. Sensors can provide those insights. The cost of sensors is continually changing, so what may not be economically practical today may be beneficial later. The other key factor is that consumers are going to learn more over time about what of their actions can be tracked and are going to expect a serious say in that tracking. Companies should get ahead of this and become part of the education process for their customers. Here is a quick overall sensors checklist to help decide how, when, and if you should consider using sensors, for both products and people.

The Sensor Checklist
Product and service tracking
Identify products that could be tracked
Identify products that should be tracked
Determine per-product tracking cost
Determine future per-product tracking cost
Determine if sensor can be used again
Plan location of sensor
Determine if there is an ecosystem to track the sensors
Check latest sensor technology
What have others done with sensors
What are others doing with sensors
Separate individual from aggregate information
Detail worst-case scenario

Customer tracking
Define customer demographics
Determine value proposition
Test value proposition with customers
Communicate, communicate, communicate
Define trackable customers
Identify customers who never want to be tracked
Separate individual from aggregate information
Define privacy policy

Define sensor ethics policy
Disclose and promote privacy policy

A slight twist in the tracking of products is that many of those products end up with consumers or in consumers' homes, which means consumers taking those products home need to be made aware – in detail – about the product tracking. As you've seen through this chapter, anything that moves can be tracked. Whether it *should* be tracked is an entirely different issue. Sensors will play a significant role in providing data that can be captured, analyzed, and converted into insights. Much of that data analyzing will occur with the help of artificial intelligence, another of the seven digital transformers discussed in the next chapter.

3 ARTIFICIAL INTELLIGENCE

Turning to the Machines

Artificial intelligence has been around in various forms for many years. However, technology and communication speeds have advanced so much in recent years that AI is at the stage of practicality for business. Advances in computing processing power along with much larger volumes of data than ever before allows the real-time crunching of mounds of data to provide new consumer services. An early example of this was when Amazon started making suggestions of what to buy, based on what one person bought compared to many others who bought the same thing. This was predictive modeling, where computers could pretty accurately predict a future behavior based on comparisons to millions of other behaviors of others. In television. Tivo did essentially the same things. The TV recording device would automatically record shows based on past viewing patterns of the consumer. More often than not, it recorded shows that the consumer did, in fact, like.

Advanced AI involves machine learning, where computers learn things without being explicitly programmed. The concept of machine learning is more than 50 years old, but the processing power and data collection capabilities of today make it increasingly more relevant and useful and companies are assembling and marketing advanced AI features today. An example of this is the Staples Easy button, which tapped IBM's Watson to become a cognitive ordering system. There's a lot of hype around artificial intelligence but there also is a lot of substance. The challenge and opportunity entails sorting out which is which. This chapter intends to help you do that.

Business Expectations

Many business leaders are interested in tapping artificial intelligence for their company, even though most are not yet using it in any form. One of the main challenges expected is how easily AI can be utilized in their business. While most business leaders are interested or even welcoming of AI into their business, the majority (69 percent) of companies are not using it. An additional 17 percent are unsure, while only 13 percent of companies say they are currently using AI.

However, AI is on the horizon for many, with 43 percent of business leaders saying their organization likely will implement any type of artificial intelligence in the next three to five years. This is according to a study comprising a survey of 200 business leaders and 200 employees from four industries: media and publishing, financial services including insurance, telecommunications including IT and corporate retail. The survey was conducted by KRC Research, a unit of the Interpublic Group, in partnership with WorkMarket. There also are differences in viewpoints between business leaders and employees. For example, while 46 percent of business leaders expect that artificial intelligence could be easily utilized in their industry or jobs, only 18 percent of employees feel the same way. Business leaders also see plenty of upsides to implementing AI.

What business leaders expect regarding AI (KRC):

- 68% -- Will enable business to determine correct cost of a specific job
- 63% -- Be widely adopted following increases in the minimum wage
- 60% -- Help business build effective teams
- 57% -- Will help business make better decisions about talent
- 51% -- Minimize the need for HR staff and hiring managers
- 39% -- Able to select workers for jobs better than humans

In all of those cases, more business leaders than employees have such expectations. Even more significantly, business leaders expect AI will have an impact across their industry and the economy.

AI expectations by business leaders (KRC):

- 72% -- Will allow me and other employees to spend more time on what matters most
- 71% -- Can help predict the spikes and slumps of customer demand
- 67% -- Will propel my company into the future
- 66% -- Will decrease labor cost through better utilization of current employees
- 64% -- Will increase productivity levels for all
- 61% -- Create a positive ripple effect across the entire global economy
- 61% -- Give my organization an edge over our competition

The number of business leaders agreeing with those statements is significantly greater than the number of employees. The most significant gap in AI deployment may be in what business leaders think compared to expectations of employees in those same organizations.

Artificial intelligence also can create a more engaging and empowering workplace, according to a different global survey. Employees would welcome AI for a number of reasons, based on the survey of 3,000 employees in eight nations conducted by The Workforce Institute at Kronos. Reasons to welcome AI include automating time-consuming internal processes (64 percent), helping balance workload (64 percent), increasing fairness in subjective decisions (62 percent) and insuring managers make better choices affecting individual employees (57 percent). The majority of organizations have not yet discussed the potential impact of AI on their workforce with employees.

"While emerging technologies always generate uncertainty, this survey shows employees worldwide share a cautious optimism that artificial intelligence is a promising tool that could pave the way for a game-changing employee experience if it is used to add fairness and eliminate low-value workplace processes and tasks, allowing employees to focus on the parts of their roles that really matter," says Joyce Maroney, executive director, The Workforce Institute at Kronos. While 82 percent of employees see an opportunity for AI to improve their jobs, a third expressed concern that it could someday replace them altogether. And AI alone won't close that divide. Another issue is the amount of buzz around the field of artificial intelligence.

Balancing the Hype and the Promise of AI

A lot of money is being invested in the Internet of Things and artificial intelligence but that doesn't mean some businesses don't see those two as being a bit overhyped. Various IoT markets show great promise, but behind all the promise is the challenge of the delivery matching expectations. Certain IoT markets are perceived to be more important than others, according to a survey of 1,500 telecommunications industry professionals conducted by Telecoms Intelligence. Most important are smart homes and smart buildings, according to the global survey.

IoT markets seen as important for companies (Telecoms Intelligence):
- 60% -- Smart home, smart building
- 53% -- Utilities
- 51% -- Healthcare
- 48% -- Smart cities
- 44% -- Logistics, asset tracking
- 43% -- Connected car
- 32% -- Retail
- 25% -- Agriculture

The Internet of Things is also at the top of the list of expected investments next year and artificial intelligence is not far behind, according to the study.

Likely priority investments (Telecoms Intelligence):
- 56% -- Internet of Things
- 46% -- Big data, analytics
- 30% -- Artificial intelligence
- 29% -- Security

While the Internet of Things and artificial intelligence are high on the list of priorities, not everyone is anticipating they will provide what is expected. Leading the list of the most overhyped emerging technologies today are the Internet of Things (20 percent) and artificial intelligence (20 percent). Next are virtual and augmented realities (15 percent) and 5G (15 percent), the next generation of mobile speed.

The good news is that 41 percent of telecom professionals think the industry's perception of IoT five years from now will be that IoT was essential to the success of telecom providers. The bad news is that 44 percent think the perception will be that IoT was useful but fell short of delivering on its initial promise. At least there's time to work on gearing up to deliver on the promise. Or, on the other side, to start refining and managing expectations. Of course, to meet the challenge of delivering on expectations, businesses will need to find the talent to make it happen.

Finding the Talent for Artificial Intelligence

In one form or another, artificial intelligence is popping up in many areas and aspects of business. With all this AI, some industries are challenged in finding qualified staff to lead their AI efforts. The most challenged industry is media and entertainment, according to a study comprising a global survey of 1,100 primary decision makers or influencer of AI technology purchases within their organization conducted by Branded Research for Infosys. Of all the industries where organization are having a tough time finding AI talent, media and entertainment is number one and the public sector is dead last.

Industries having difficult time finding qualified staff to lead AI initiatives (Branded Research):
- 68% -- Media and entertainment
- 67% -- Telecom, communication service providers

- 66% -- Banking and insurance
- 62% -- Retail and consumer product goods
- 61% -- Healthcare
- 60% -- Travel, hospitality and transportation
- 56% -- Manufacturing and high tech
- 41% -- Public sector

Numerous industries are being impacted by artificial intelligence, according to the study. For example, the majority (54 percent) of retailers are experiencing disruption due to AI technologies, along with 53 percent of media and entertainment companies and 48 percent of those in travel, hospitality and transportation. In terms of using AI to automate business processes, 85 percent of retail and consumer product goods companies take the top spot above all other industries. Artificial intelligence will find its way into all industries. Now if those industries can just find the people to help lead it along. As AI in business grows, more jobs will be created and ultimately, results will start to be measured.

Companies Invest, Look for Results

Now that various forms of artificial intelligence are getting a workout in real-life markets, data is emerging highlighting some of the ups and downs. Early adopters of AI report strong opportunities, according to one view, while another study points to the need for changes in current processes. The majority (76 percent) of executives in 'cognitive aware' companies expect AI to transform their organization while most (69 percent) anticipate minimal or no job losses. The study, comprising a survey of 250 U.S. executives conducted by Deloitte, found that almost a third (29 percent) of businesses see the addition of new jobs being created along with the adoption of AI. However, there are some potential pitfalls ahead, at least for some departments.

The reality is that deploying artificial intelligence is hardly a simple undertaking. The majority (55 percent) of businesses deploying AI have not received any tangible business outcomes and 43 percent say it is too soon to tell, based on a study by Forrester. That study, comprising a survey of 3,400 executives in 10 countries, found that the majority (51 percent) of companies are investing in AI, an increase from 40 percent the previous year. The study suggests that unless firms plan, deploy, and govern it correctly, new AI tech will provide only meager benefits or even unexpected and undesired results. One reason to get AI right: 73 percent of execs say that being highly responsive to rising customer expectations is one of their top priorities over the next year. Artificial intelligence, done right, can help them do that, and many businesses are pursuing various forms of artificial intelligence.

Different Levels of Artificial Intelligence

Artificial intelligence may mean different things to different people, but that isn't stopping some businesses from moving full steam ahead with it. AI has become somewhat of an umbrella term covering a range of technologies, including natural language processing, machine learning, computer vision, and deep learning, among others. Intelligent assistants like Amazon's Alexa, Apple's Siri, Microsoft's Cortana, and Google's Home all are viewed as using AI, to one degree or another.

There are different levels of AI, with the most common today dealing with a computer's superior ability to process large amounts of data and find patterns. Most (85 percent) executives involved in technology say AI has lived up to its promises, although 76 percent are concerned that over-optimistic marketing will make it difficult to vet AI-powered solutions, according to a study comprising a survey of 650 technology decision makers in the U.S., U.K., Germany and France conducted by Market Cube for Cylance. Most (83 percent) execs say they invest in AI to beat the competition and more than 70 percent say AI has changed how marketing departments operate. After many years, practical AI is coming of age, with 60 percent of companies having at least some form of AI deployed, according to the survey.

Rather than replacing workers, 81 percent of tech execs see AI as leading to more meaningful work for employees and almost all (93 percent) anticipating that AI will create new types of jobs. Money is also flowing toward AI, with more than a third (38 percent) of businesses planning to spend one-fourth to one-half of their entire technical budget on AI within the next we months. Some of the top benefits expected to come from AI are increased insight into customer behavior, boosted business performance, automation of repetitive tasks and improvements to operational efficiency, according to the study. The potential big payoff for marketers is that increased customer insight, typically among the benefits found in every AI study, although there still will be some bumps in the road.

AI in Product Innovation

The adoption of artificial intelligence is well underway, but many executives expect some roadblocks ahead. There's a lot of enthusiasm and optimism for AI, most notably as a potential competitive advantage. For example, after deploying AI for various online advertising functions, lingerie retailer Cosabella learned plenty of lessons and adapted and modified from there.

Any business that doesn't start using AI in at least some area will be missing that learning and find themselves behind.

The good news is that most (80 percent) large businesses have some form of AI in use within their organization, although many see room for improvement. A survey of 260 business and technology decision-makers of vice president level or higher in the Americas, Europe and Asia-Pacific who work for companies with revenue of $50 million or more, found that while most (83 percent) business in the Americas have some form of AI capabilities in use, 44 percent of them say there is lots of room for further implementation and other integration. The study was conducted by research firm Vanson Bourne for Teradata.

The top areas where businesses are driving revenue with AI are product innovation (50 percent) and customer service (46 percent). Almost a third (32 percent) are seeing AI driving revenue in marketing. In the Americas, the leading department driving revenue from AI capabilities is customer service and the top three areas in the Americas that will drive business outcomes are customer experience (62 percent), operational excellence (56 percent) and product innovation (51 percent).

There are perceived barriers along the way, most notably lack of infrastructure, lack of access to talent and understanding, and AI technology being still nascent and unproven, according to the survey. Artificial intelligence is coming into businesses of all types and categories in a big way and where it starts is just the beginning of a journey. The key is that many AI functions will end up impacting consumers in many ways, since much of the AI focus on business ends up being aimed at their customers, and that's where AI in customer service comes in.

Teaching AI for Better Customer Service

More companies are deploying various forms of artificial intelligence and it looks like many customers aren't going to be all that happy about it. As companies optimize their customer service approaches, chatbots will increasingly become alternatives to email. And as they look to reduce costs and headcount in contact centers, more businesses will push customers to digital and chatbots, according to an AI forecast by Forrester. The bad news is that the transition to AI will be somewhat bumpy, which will have a negative impact of customer satisfaction, according to the Forrester forecast.

Companies will increasingly apply AI to specific customer-facing channels, discovering that machine learning often requires a highly manual process of categorizing text, speech, or visual customer interactions not recognized by AI technology. Essentially, the machines will have to be taught some of the things they don't yet know. This early form of blending technology with the correct amount of human-assisted processes to improve machine learning will be a big disruptor, according to the forecast. Among the Forrester predictions relating to artificial intelligence:

- Several major brands will kill customer service email in favor of chatbots and chat. Major brands will start to favor real-time communications via chat and chatbots rather than through mobile apps and email in websites.
- Companies will use visual sentiment analysis to improve service and sales outcomes. Facial recognition will be used to gauge emotion and sentiment, a technological capability that will be extended to customer service and sales.
- At least one B2B firm will conduct more than 50 percent of its lead nurturing with AI. Conversational

AI will start to automate more of the lead processes, reducing the cost of a sale, enabling sellers to focus more on the most qualified leads.

All of this movement into more automated processes will cause service levels and customer satisfaction to suffer, due to management expectations of AI automation. This will lead to customer service numbers being harder to locate on corporate websites and in apps, since the companies will want to route customers through technology rather than dealing with them directly, which is more expensive, according to the Forrester predictions.

While artificial intelligence in various forms of virtual assistants has caught the eye of many in business, its adoption by marketing leaders may be a bit lagging. Only seven percent of marketing decision-makers say they are using AI-powered chatbots, according to a survey of 500 senior marketers worldwide, with most based in the U.S. or U.K. The study was conducted by ClickZ for Freedman International. About a quarter (27 percent) of marketers say it is something they plan to think about. The most popular reasons for not using artificial intelligence are internal teams not being ready for it and not having the budget. A relatively small number (13 percent) of marketers say their customers are not ready for AI.

Deploying AI solutions can have great long-term benefits. The risk is that companies don't devote enough resource to getting it right before counting on the returns. However, some companies make AI investments early and often.

Italian Lingerie Brand Cosabella Taps AI

One global luxury brand is tapping AI for everything from ad buys to personalized promotions. Cosabella, a global lingerie brand headquartered in Italy, transformed how it interacts with customers with AI-driven targeted advertising spending. Using an artificial intelligence system called Albert, Cosabella increased its global customer reach, identifying new customers in various countries around the world.

"AI creates a lot of efficiencies," Guido Campello, CEO of Cosabella tells me. "We applied AI to our ad spend and now we're focused on how we scale it." Cosabella put Albert in charge of advertising spending and uses AI for personalized email promotions. "We replaced our email marketing pretty quickly," says Campello. Using Albert converted the programs into one of constant evolution.

Now that various systems are automated via the AI of Albert, Cosabella is essentially re-balancing. "We're bringing people back into the process," says Campello. "It's about getting the right mix of people and technology. "AI needs the human element in our category, since trends and forecasts are not necessarily predictable. There are so many variables and factors."

Adding AI into the company processes also drove some internal changes. "We took the marketing and digital department spends and merged them together," says Campello.

Albert has helped Cosabella to buy ads based on identifying and leveraging the best search words, though is somewhat challenged by discovering future words. "That requires a mix of human and IA," says Campello. The first phase of using Albert was basically to let the AI do its thing. "I hate saying this, but it's like having an agency in a box," says Or Shani, CEO and founder of Albert. "Brands bring their creative assets, tell Albert the goals and set a budget. But at the end of the day, Albert is a machine and that machine measures results as it goes. "In reality, machine learning is only needed with a problem that is so complex, like the synchronization of messaging, that there needs to be machine learning. Brands come to us not because they want to use AI, but because they want to solve a problem. Five to 10 years from now, everyone is going to use this type of solution." Shani views Albert as part of a team rather than simply a tool. Cosabella tends to agree. Campello says the internal team, being Italian, even refers to the AI engine as *Alberto*. It's not only Italian lingerie brands that get that artificial intelligence is a mega trend in business.

AI in Wearables

Artificial intelligence and voice are coming to wearables as the devices get tuned to much more specific uses. Companies are starting to tap AI to give consumers actionable information for fitness wearables, according to a new fitness wearables study. Fitness devices also are expanding, with strong growth in clothing and ear-based fitness wearables projected. The shipment of such devices will grow 60 percent a year over the next four years, according to the report by Juniper Research.

This means specialized wearable devices will account for 25 percent of the market within four years. Wearables began with fitness trackers and then branched out into more sophisticated devices, most notably the Apple Watch, though not in the category of fitness trackers. Fitness trackers basically became *smarter* over time, providing health measures, such as steps taken, heart rate and oxygenation.

The ongoing challenge for fitness trackers is continued usage. For example, fewer than 60 percent of registered users of Fitbit devices are classed as active users in any given year, according to the study. Going forward, there are three elements a fitness wearable must have to succeed, according to the report by Juniper Research.

- Multiple metrics – Tracking numerous metrics, such as heart rate, calorie burn, distance, location and step counting, will be required and made possible by the miniaturization of a range of sensors that can feed more information into a system.

- Artificial intelligence – Some companies are promoting their products as having AI, leading to the analytics platform being the primary offering of wearables. The data platform is projected to become more important to consumers than the device.

- Targeted fitness – Several wearables now target more precise uses, such as smart running shoes, biometric-tracking hearables and specialist running smartwatches. These types of devices are not intended to be constantly worn and are likely to be higher priced.

One of the most significant expectations from AI being used in wearables is the addition of voice-based advice on training techniques, according to Juniper. This advice is expected to be delivered via hearables. Voice is entering yet another area of the Internet of Things.

AI in Elevators

Even through the Internet of Things can involve devices or machines *talking* to each other, the *conversation* is generally silent. No more. In a rather offbeat twist, an ad agency has given voice to elevators, so they can have conversations in real time, allowing people to hear machines talk. Hasan and Partners, the Finland agency, formerly part of IPG, had a long-time global elevator client that wanted to more easily describe its elevator monitoring capabilities. "As an ad agency, we wanted to show the world that Kone has a world-leading elevator service," Tobias Wacker, creative director at Hasan and Partners in Finland says. The agency worked with Kone to connect selected elevators in different countries around the world. The elevators send data from sensors and controls about their day-to-day performance. That data, basically computer code, is collected, processed and given a voice. Literally.

Anyone can go online and hear the elevator speak. The elevators that speak are in Sweden, Illinois, Finland, and France and all are translated into English. Wacker says the agency used IBM Watson's text-to-speech system and all the speaking is in real time. "It's real data in real time," says Wacker. "Everything is real." The approach was taken to introduce a new level of service of elevator maintenance. "This connects elevators to the cloud, so nobody needs to call for repairs in the future," Wacker says. "AI and the Internet of Things is so hot right now that we wanted to do our part to show the world that this is what the Internet of Things means." This is an actual conversation, by voice I heard, from an elevator in Illinois. The 'conversation' is between the elevator and the Kone cloud:

"On my way down to floor 0."

I confirm

Please verify landing accuracy on floor 6

No worries, near perfect

Just rode 8.1 meters down to floor 4

I copy, you're on floor 4

On my way down to floor 3

Roger. That's down to floor 3

Speed 1.4 m/s

Received

Minimal bounce while landing on floor 3

Measured, good landing

Please verify external noise level

Measuring…slightly elevated

Noticed vibration while going up

A bit, yes. Analyzing

Ready to ride

Wait for passengers

Slight vibration on the way up

Measured as below average

Highly accurate landing on floor 4

Good job
Slight vibration on the way down
Measured. Hardly noticeable

Conversations started by an elevator may not be the most exciting, but they do bring to life the concept of machine-to-machine communication. "The Information is in real time, so we can't really dramatize it," says Wacker. Making elevators speak may actually be enough.

IBM Goes All in on AI

The Internet of Things is about connections and the massive amounts of data that result from those connections. Trouble is, most of the resulting data is not tapped, and that's where IBM and its AI mega-machine Watson come in. During a break in the IBM Genius of Things summit in Boston, I sat down with Harriet Green, general manager of Watson IoT and customer engagement and education at IBM, to discuss IBM's IoT and AI strategy.

Green sees a market need as an opportunity, noting that 80 percent of the world's data is not yet searchable. "We've made a big bet ($3 billion) on IoT and bringing AI capabilities to IoT," says Green. "We're seeing this huge drive to connect the world's devices to, in our case, the IBM cloud, the IoT platform. People are understanding that if you connect things to things and things to people, the data flows and the opportunities are very real. "Secondly, we're seeing that the software application to gather this data and apply analytics to it are becoming deeper and richer. We're seeing many more outcomes."

The volume and speed of processing data by AI engines far surpasses human capabilities and unexpected correlations or insights often are discovered as a result. IBM's Watson approach is to use the AI technology to augment or add to what a company or organization is doing. Various iterations of AI have been around for many years but have been maturing in recent years due to additional processing power and learnings along the way. "IBM has been working with and investing in Watson for 10 years and so much has been developed since Jeopardy," says Green. (Watson famously won the game back in 2011.)

"The critical thing is that in none of our work do we think about replacing human intelligence. We believe that Watson is working together and augmenting that human capability with the Watson intelligence, which keeps learning from what it's given. I think many, many jobs in the world will be changed by the advent of artificial intelligence, but I think this suggestion that there will be mass displacement, we have not seen that. This year, more than a billion people will be touched by Watson."

IBM says it has 6,000 active clients from 30 different industries using its IoT platform and Watson. There also are plenty of examples of AI coming in contact with consumers, even if consumers don't necessarily look at the experience as being driven by artificial intelligence. Some examples cited by Green:

- "Olli, the self-driving car, will take you from point A to point B, provide recommendations on restaurants you might like, remind you to get to your destination at a given time and now, with weather conditions, is enabled by Watson. That is being expanded across school routes in many, many states and the school children will queue to be on the Olli rather than a boring old bus that doesn't talk to them.
- "BMW is injecting Watson AI capabilities into its i8 hybrid sports car."

- Kone, the global elevator company that moves 1 million people a day, is an example of real-time connectivity, as mentioned previously. Elevators in Finland, Illinois, Sweden and France are all connected to the cloud and communicate from elevator to cloud. Any consumer can tap in and actually hear elevators speak.

- While many AI applications are being deployed by large, global companies, many of the results end up impacting consumers at various stages of their daily lives.

"Most consumers have interactions with enterprises," says Green. "What I see happening here is a real convergence in behaviors, from what consumers see in enterprises, and know what is possible, and what enterprises can deliver to various consumers. A large part of the IoT future entails new products and services that quantifiably do things smarter, better, provide a richer experience and a new experience. These are very exciting times. It's very important that we all stay focused on what really adds value, quantifiable benefit and get started." Green and her team clearly know where their focus is. Artificial intelligence is finding its ways into all areas of business, even in the research and testing arena.

AI in A/B Testing

Having been around since forever, A/B testing may not be fading away, but thanks to advances in artificial intelligence, it may be moving more to the back of the line. At the eTail East conference and exhibition in Boston, the exhibition hall was filled with companies promoting countless versions of data analytics, customer targeting and, most prominently, various promises of AI-driven results. One of the standouts, with some solid AI conversion case studies, was San Francisco based Sentient, a 10-year-old AI company that uses a branch of artificial intelligence called evolutionary algorithms. I sat down with Jeremy Miller, director of marketing at Sentient, to discuss the current status and potential future of the old world of A/B testing in relation to the new world of AI.

"In traditional A/B testing formats, you have your control vs. an experiment," says Miller. "You run that experiment against your traffic and whichever design performs better is the one you deploy, which is pretty much the tried and true practice. "But people have found that six out of seven experiments don't result in a positive outcome, so you actually have to put a lot of energy and resources to try to determine how you can actually increase conversions using A/B testing."

Sentient's conversion-focused product called Ascend lets marketers test all their ideas simultaneously instead of in a linear, sequential way. "With evolutionary algorithms, it mimics the process of evolution. It takes all of those ideas and does continuous optimization," Miller says. "The marketers can give the AI all of their ideas, and then based on the traffic that comes to their site, it starts to understand which ideas increase conversions better. The ones that increase conversions better get to live on and the ones that do not convert better get pruned away and do not get to live on."

Conversion could be any metric determined by the brand or marketer, such as getting a lead, making a sale or a meeting a revenue goal. It's basically an end goal determined that's handed off to the AI engine, which then determines how to meet that goal. In one case for Cosabella, the global luxury lingerie brand, the Sentient AI engine tested 160-page designs and the AI evolved over seven weeks ending in a 38 percent improvement in conversions. "In two or three years, everyone is going to take advantage of AI," Miller says. Despite results like these, A/B testing is not likely going away any time soon.

"A/B testing is confirmatory," Miller says. "If you're looking to confirm a hypothesis, an A/B test can still provide some value. "You may have a strong hypothesis and you want to see if it is correct, then A/B is a method of doing that. It's not exploration. It's already predetermined what you think is correct and you're just validating or invalidating. When you're exploring, you're really navigating toward the highest possible conversion. You're exploring all the way up the mountain to get to the highest peak vs. just this local peak, which an A/B test really gets you. You might get lucky with A/B testing, but you didn't allow for the possibility that something else could have allowed it to be better." Sentient's AI just eliminates the issue of hoping to be lucky. Besides research, the world of retail is also getting a dose of AI.

Retail AI for Customer Engagement

Retailers are buying into artificial intelligence with the expectation that it will improve customer engagement. Many marketing executives also look at engagement as impacting revenue and driving purchases. The majority (86 percent) of retailers plan to invest in AI or machine learning and 69 percent already use it in their marketing organization, according to a study comprising interviews of 100 CMOs and senior marketing executives at major brands headquartered in the U.S. and U.K. Companies surveyed included Best Buy, Marks and Spencer, Urban Outfitters, Williams-Sonoma, and Nordstrom, among others. The study was conducted by Worldwide Business Research (WBR) and Persado.

The amount of investment in AI and machine learning by retail marketers is substantial. The majority (66 percent) of marketers have budgeted from $1 million to $100 million, with 19 percent of those budgeting between $50 million and $100 million. Most marketing execs expect AI to have a direct impact on top-line growth.

Expected benefits of AI and machine leaning in marketing (Persado):

- 86% -- More effective in terms of engagement
- 80% -- Stay ahead of competition
- 70% -- Risk management, data security
- 69% -- Drive systematic uplifts in campaigns
- 53% -- Increase productivity and efficiencies

Even with all the positive expectations, many retailers have some issue with AI. For example, the majority are confused or not trusting of the technology.

Biggest roadblocks to retail AI adoption (Persado):

- 76% -- Confusion or lack of clarity for what AI can be used for
- 59% -- Distrust of introducing AI technology
- 52% -- Lack of defined business case
- 46% -- Lack of appropriate skills in-house
- 29% -- Lack of management buy-in
- 18% -- Don't' have time, resource

On the positive site, retailers are investing in AI, which should lead to the resolution of some of the roadblocks. Those who don't will continue to face those obstacles.

AI for Product Recommendations

Online retailers are moving into some advanced artificial intelligence technologies while holding back on others. Many retailers have concrete plans for using artificial intelligence for various customer-facing activities, but they don't have plans for virtual reality or even voice-activated apps. Using augmented reality also is near the bottom of the list, based a survey of 234 mid-size online retail merchants globally conducted by SLI Systems, an ecommerce company. The top planned retailer use for AI is for personalized product recommendations.

Uses of AI by retailers (SLS Systems):

- 56% -- Personalized product recommendations
- 41% -- Customer service requests
- 35% -- Chatbots
- 32% -- Visual search
- 18% -- Virtual buying assistants
- 11% -- Augmented reality
- 8% -- Voice-activated apps
- 7% -- Virtual reality

Most (90 percent) online retailers have no short-term plans to use AI for virtual reality or voice-activated apps and the majority (54 percent) plan to at least eventually use AI, with almost half (46 percent) with no plans to add it to their commerce strategy.

Some (16 percent) retailers already use some form of AI, with 20 percent planning to add it in the short term and 18 percent planning to add it in the longer term. Like many technologies relatively new to a market, learning what it can do is key. Almost a quarter (24 percent) of retailers say they don't understand how AI can be applied to commerce and while more than a third (39 percent) say they understand AI's commerce applications, they weren't sure how it applied to their businesses.

Marketers and AI

Marketers are looking to artificial intelligence in a big way, since it is the leading technology that they expect to grow the most in the near future. Marketers expect AI will grow by 53 percent, higher than any other technology type, according to the State of Marketing Report, comprising a survey of 3,500 marketing leaders globally conducted by Salesforce Research**Error! Bookmark not defined.**. The majority (51 percent) of marketing leaders already using AI and more than a quarter plan to at least do an AI pilot in the next two years. Of the marketers already using AI, most (64 percent) say it has increased their overall marketing efficiency and more than half (57 percent) say it is essential to help them create one-to-one marketing. There are many areas where marketing leaders see AI having a major impact on their business.

AI impact over the next 5 years (Salesforce Error! Bookmark not defined. **Research):**
- 61% -- Hyper-personalization of content
- 61% -- Dynamic landing pages and websites
- 61% -- Delivering the right message, on the right channel at the right time
- 60% -- Hyper-personalized product recommendations
- 60% -- Programmatic advertising and media buying
- 60% -- Predictive journeys
- 59% -- Productivity of marketers
- 59% -- Campaign analytics
- 59% -- Digital asset management
- 59% -- Business insights across data and systems
- 59% -- Hyper-personalization at scale
- 58% -- Customer segmentation
- 57% -- Lead scoring
- 56% -- Sentiment analysis

Despite all of this, it doesn't mean there's AI smooth sailing ahead. A separate Salesforce**Error! Bookmark not defined.** survey found that only 26 percent of business leaders, including marketing, sales and service, have complete confidence in their organization's ability to define an AI business strategy. Obstacles to executing an AI strategy include customer privacy concerns, sorting out data stored in separate systems, budget constraints and internal skills. Other than that, all AI systems are go.

AI in Personal Finances

Many consumers see artificial intelligence as a way to help them manage their money. From finding loans and creating a budget to devising savings strategies and getting unbiased advice, AI is viewed as a potentially big help. One study suggests that AI could be helpful in managing finances and do a number of things better than consumers. The study comprised a survey of 1,000 U.S. adults conducted by Propeller Insights for Varo Money, a banking app company. There are some things consumers think AI can do better than them.

Where AI assistant could do better (Varo Money):
- 50% -- Creating a budget
- 44% -- Managing money
- 44% -- Saving money
- 32% -- Predicting bad weather
- 19% -- Driving a car
- 9% -- Being funny

Consumers also say they would take advantage of various artificial intelligence features if their mobile banking had them.

Consumers would take advantage of (Varo Money):
- 42% -- Automatically paying bills

- 39% -- Analyzing cash flow
- 37% -- Connecting bank accounts, credit cards, loans in one place
- 34% -- Transferring money between accounts
- 29% -- Faster debt repayment
- 28% -- Setting categorized savings goals
- 23% -- Finding a loan
- 16% -- Preventing insolvency

More millennials than others would take advantage of features, such as automatic spending analysis (41 percent), analyzing cash flow (47 percent) and connecting bank accounts (42 percent). One interesting tidbit found in the survey: 7 percent of consumers visit a physical bank branch only once in a six-month period, 5 percent once in a year and 10 percent never visit. Besides banking, the exploration of artificial intelligence continues, especially at many universities.

AI and Spotting Lying

One of the most powerful aspects of artificial intelligence is that it can see things that humans can't. More precisely, it can analyze data and find previously unseen correlations, some likely never to be discovered manually on a recurring basis. Now researchers are tapping AI to tell if a person is lying, such as in a courtroom trial. The system for covert automated deception detection, named DARE (Deception Analysis Reasoning Engine), is an AI engine that uses video features that detect human micro-expressions.

Researchers from the University of Maryland and Dartmouth College use real-life courtroom trial videos. Their system uses classifiers trained on video features that predict human micro-expressions, which they determined could be used to predict deception. The researchers created a three-step process involving capturing audio and video and then data encoding. They trained their AI engine to identify the five most predictive micro-expressions: frowning, eyebrows raising, lip corners up, lips protruded and head side turn.

The researchers created a database of trial video clips, with 50 truthful videos and 54 that were deceptive. They then had 15 people watch the videos and the DARE system ended up being more accurate than the people in predicting when someone in the video was lying. The AI engine detected deception at a rate of 92 percent.

Artificial intelligence can combine audio, video, and transcriptions in real-time to make a determination. It can see and process more things simultaneously and conclude which statements are likely not true, with a high degree of accuracy. In the future, it may be difficult to lie to AI. Meantime, many consumers are warming to the idea of artificial intelligence, especially noting the potential to solve major issues.

Consumers Have High Hopes for AI

Consumers are rooting for AI, but many also see some potential problems. Artificial intelligence is viewed as a way to solve issues ranging from those related to cybersecurity and privacy to global education, according to a survey of a nationally representative sample of 2,500 U.S. consumers and business decision makers aimed at exploring attitudes towards artificial intelligence conducted by PwC. Participants were screened for basic familiarity with AI. PwC notes that artificial intelligence today works in three ways:

- Assisted intelligence -- Widely available now, improves what people and organizations already do. An example is a car GPS navigation program that offers directions and adjusts to road conditions.

- Augmented intelligence – Emerging, enables people and organizations to do things they couldn't otherwise do. One example would be the combination of programs that organize cars in ride-sharing services.
- Autonomous intelligence, being developed for the future, establishes machines that act on their own. An example would be self-driving vehicles, when they come into widespread use.

The majority (63 percent) of consumers say AI will help solve complex problems that plague modern societies and 59 percent say it will help people live more fulfilling lives. On the other hand, almost half (46 percent) believe AI will harm people by taking jobs away and 23 percent say it will have serious negative implications. However, there's a slight twist to viewpoints on jobs:

- 80 percent say it's more important to have access to more affordable legal advice than to preserve the jobs of lawyers
- 69 percent would rather have more affordable, convenient and reliable transportation than preserve the jobs of taxi drivers
- 64 percent would rather have instant access to quality customer service than preserve the jobs of customer service reps

Digital assistants are leading the first wave of artificial intelligence adoption, according to the PwC study. The majority (72 percent) of business execs already are using digital assistants, as are 53 percent of millennials and 42 percent of consumers. More than a third (34 percent) of business execs say that the time freed up by using digital assistants allows them to focus on deep thinking and creating.

Consumers seem to have big hopes for AI. The majority (66 percent) see it being involved in curing cancer and diseases,

68 percent for help solving issues relating to cybersecurity and privacy and 58 percent in helping with global education.

Another PwC study, the 2018 Global Consumer Insights Survey of 22,000 consumers in 27 territories around the world found that AI adoption differs by region. The study also showed that while artificial intelligence continues to improve in devices like smart speakers, it doesn't mean consumers want it. The majority of consumers don't yet have any AI devices and most people have no interest in owning them, based on the study. Device ownership varies by country, but overall, 10 percent of consumers own an AI device, 32 percent plan to get one and most (58 percent) say they have no interest.

In the U.S., AI-device ownership is at 16 percent with an additional 25 percent planning to acquire an AI device, such as Amazon Echo or Google Home.

AI-ownership level of the top 10 countries (PwC):

- 21% -- China
- 19% -- Vietnam
- 18% -- Indonesia
- 16% -- U.S.
- 15% -- Thailand
- 14% -- Brazil
- 14% -- France
- 14% -- U.K.
- 13% -- Poland
- 13% -- Italy

The overall picture is likely to change, based on the number of people who plan to get an AI-device in the future. Brazil (59 percent), China (52 percent) and Indonesia (49 percent) lead. Early adopters of AI devices are most likely men aged 18 to 34. They are more likely to shop via mobile on a daily and weekly basis, pay by mobile payment, more comfortable shopping online and less likely to take action to minimize risk of security issues and fraud. Female device ownership is at 9 percent with 27 percent planning to purchase and 64 percent having no interest. Male ownership is at 12 percent, with 36 percent planning to buy and 52 percent having no interest. Among consumers with an AI device, almost half (48 percent) spend the same amount on shopping as they did previously and 18 percent spend more. Ownership and AI-device behaviors are going to evolve as the technology evolves as well. For example, smart speakers will get 'smarter' and ultimately become more useful for consumer activities. These are still the early days of the Internet of Things and AI has some big hopes and expectations to deal with.

Dive in to AI

As you saw in this chapter, artificial intelligence is all over the business landscape in one form or another. Business leaders are open to it, though some aren't necessarily sure which direction to head. One way to think about AI is that there are two essential places for it: internally and externally. Artificial intelligence can be used internally to automate processes, streamline tasks, and aid in complex decision-making. Externally, AI can be used to improve customer service, especially by providing the right answers to consumers or quickly routing them to the right person or place to help. Artificial intelligence can be very good at sorting through masses of data and finding key insights that a person is not likely to quickly identify. However, artificial intelligence does not replace human thinking, creativity, and instincts. Luxury retailer Cosabella found that out after it highly automated certain process using artificial intelligence and then added people back into the mix, as discussed earlier in this chapter. Among other things, artificial intelligence can help deal with masses of data that many organizations are accumulating freeing them to focus on more things that matter.

Artificial intelligence can help an organization better serve customers. One example of this is in the explosion of chatbots. While many companies are rushing to deploy chatbots, it's good to remember that some people still want to talk to a real person, while others expect automated technology will better serve them. Businesses need to provide the capability for both of those customer sets to be identified on-the-fly and routed appropriately. That will make for more happy customers. These are some other aspects to consider:

- **Allocate resource.** The start of the intelligence for an artificial intelligence deployment involves teaching the technology what it is that is desired and what kind of data it has to work with. This means people have to decide what it is that will go into the system and then help it *learn* over time. The more humans help the automating machinery, the better it will get. AI is not a set-it-and-forget-it deployment.

- **Clean the data.** The old saying garbage-in, garbage-out applies more to artificial intelligence than to anything else. Bad, incomplete, or inaccurate data will not provide a good result, not matter how good the AI engine is. This is the AI starting point.

- **Allow time.** An AI engine is not built overnight, at least not one that provides desired results. In addition to resources, especially staffing, the results take time. Keep in mind there will be more costs before more results.

- **Don't go it alone.** There are companies that are very good at deploying artificial intelligence solutions, some mentioned earlier in this chapter. Do your homework and check out the leaders. They likely have more dedicated resources than most (but not all) companies and they continually improve the technology, since that is what they do.

One of the seven digital transformers that is growing with artificial intelligence is voice. Many smart voice assistants are learning as they go, which we deal with in the next chapter.

4 VOICE ASSISTANTS

Speaking to the Machines

The growth of digital voice assistant devices in the home is explosive. The market was kicked off in earnest with the introduction of Amazon's digital assistant Alexa, showcased in Amazon's Echo line of products. Amazon followed with its Google Home line, so that millions of consumers found themselves in their kitchen, living room, or bedroom, saying "Hey Alexa" or "Hey Google," followed by their request-of-the-moment. Others joined in, such as Apple with its HomePod smart speaker and while Samsung and its Harman division work with Samsung's voice agent Bixby. Voice control ultimately will be built into countless devices, but this chapter deals primarily with standalone digital voice assistants, the most significant area of voice assistants.

However, there's more to voice assistants than just having them recognize a question. "As people talk about Alexa in their home and with these other smart speakers coming out, everyone's very floored by how good the recognition quality is," says Tom Hebner, worldwide leader of the cognitive innovation group at Nuance Communications, a 14,000-

employee global company whose speech solutions support up to 80 different languages. "For me, it's much more about how much it solved my problem versus how good the recognition is," he tells me during a lengthy conversation.

One of the best uses of voice assistants is to help solve problems. Asking home voice assistants a quick question or having them turn something on or off are simple examples. Many consumers have come across other types of voice assistants when they may be trying to reach a company for one reason or another, often to solve an issue.

"We are looking at all of our conversational tech, even the virtual assistants, and when we do satisfaction surveys, the happiest people are the ones that solve the problems with automation and that's because it's fast," says Hebner. "What people want is to have their problem solved quickly and they don't necessarily care if it's through a human or with automation, as long as it's done quickly. The people who are the most frustrated are the ones that take a long time in any kind of automated system and then get to a person and then have to go to multiple people to solve their problem. Those are the most frustrating, because it took the most time and the most effort on their part. In terms of the people, the happiest they're going to be is when their problem is solved quickly. Those people screaming 'agent' at their phones are because those phone systems weren't designed well and had the perception of being in the way of the person versus solving their problem. If you have a well-designed system that solves their problem, or quickly escalates them to a human, they're not going to feel like they're blocked, they're going to feel like they're progressing."

No matter the voice assistant, solving customer problems can easily come up as an issue. "We are looking at all of our conversational tech, even the virtual assistants, and when we do satisfaction surveys, the happiest people are the ones that solve the problems with automation, and that's because it's fast," says Hebner. "That's where conversational design becomes very important, because how you design that experience, how you build that experience for those people, will determine and strongly influence their behavior."

Voice assistants also rely on data, since they have to quickly pull from a pool to answer queries quickly and accurately. "If I was the CIO of a large company right now, I would make sure our data is accessible, make sure it's available, make sure that every one of our front ends can use it," says Hebner. "AI is only as good as the data you feed it, which people say a lot. They'll say they've built machine learning models off of poor data and they perform poorly. We've barely scratched the surface. It's an exciting time." The good news is that for consumers at home, the problems being handed to smart speakers may not yet be highly challenging, since both consumers and smart speakers are at the learning stage. The smart home speaker market is still relatively new, but the devices are becoming a key component of the smart home.

Smart Speakers Drive Smart Homes

The number of smart home devices continues to rise, and it's projected that there will be 800 million in the U.S. within four years. The size of the smart home market is being pushed along quite nicely by smart speaker adoption, with 55 billion overall IoT devices installed around the world by 2025, according to a study by BI Intelligence. The smart speaker market is dominated by Amazon's Echo and Google's Home lines of product, but Amazon and Google are not alone in the market. Microsoft launched a smart speaker called Invoke for its Cortana voice assistant, Samsung's Harman-Kardon is dialing in with Samsung's Bixby voice assistant, and Apple joined the smart home speaker market with the launch of its pricey HomePod smart speaker. We agree with BI Intelligence that smart speakers will gradually transform into one of many peripheral devices around the central voice assistant.

Smart speakers are also a driver for more smart home products, since they can relatively easily control other smart devices, such as lights and thermostats, and several at time, which is discussed in detail in another chapter. Smart home devices still appeal more to tech-savvy consumers but are starting to move to average users, according to the study. Companies are looking to attract early adopters to try their devices, essentially relying on them for free marketing to others, since early adopters tend to show off their devices to friends and family, according to the study. At least early adopters now have more smart speakers entering the market, making their job easier. In addition to playing music, smart speakers create a hands-free environment for consumers to do things in their homes.

Benefits of Voice Assistants

There are two sides to smart home voice assistants. While consumers flock to the devices, including Alexa, Google Assistant, Siri, and Bixby, the expected benefits ride along with a bevy of concerns. The top benefit of smart home voice assistants is the hands-free capability provided, while the top concern is a lack of trust in security, based on a BI Intelligence study, comprising a survey of 900 millennials and business leaders in a U.S. panel who make strategic decision within their organizations. A certain number (18 percent) of people don't see a reason to have a home voice assistant, but a large majority (83 percent) do.

Main benefits of home voice assistant (BI Intelligence):

- 33% -- Hands-free home control
- 20% -- It's futuristic and fun
- 15% -- Versatile connected speaker
- 10% -- Perform multiple tasks at once
- 5% -- Other

However, there are a number of potential pitfalls for voice assistants. For example, many consumers worry about their security. Part of that concern is likely driven by outward security measures, such as a lack of requirement to put in a password or verify identity. Basically, Alexa will communicate with anyone. In addition, some (19 percent) consumers see a drawback as an anticipated negative experience due to technology issues. A small number (11 percent) of consumers don't see any drawbacks.

Drawbacks of home voice assistant (BI Intelligence):

- 41% -- Don't trust it to be secure
- 19% - Too buggy
- 12% -- Too expensive
- 9% -- Don't see a use
- 9% -- Other

Voice assistance will continue to improve over time, as will the 'intelligence' behind them. One of the promises of the Internet of Things is the expansion of hands-free interactions. Some of these will be triggered by location sensors and others by gestures or biometric methods. However, one of the main causes of interactions will be by voice and the smart home voice assistants are the beginning of that.

Another study found that almost all consumers at least are aware of smart speakers -- but that doesn't necessarily mean they know a lot about them or what they do. While almost all (95 percent) consumers have heard of smart speakers, one in five (20 percent) don't know much about them, based on the study, comprising a survey of 4,000 U.S. and U.K. consumers conducted by Delineate, a research and insights agency based in the U.K.

Why they use smart speakers (BI Intelligence):

- 12% -- Learn something
- 11% -- Research a brand, company
- 11% -- Entertainment, fun
- 10% -- Check facts
- 10% -- Follow the news
- 9% -- Help choose a brand or product
- 8% -- Follow celebrities

Traditional searches on PCs and phones still are significantly larger, but the trend is clear. Key for marketers is that almost one in 10 consumers (9 percent in the U.S., 7 percent in the U.K.) are already using smart speakers to help them decide on brands and products.

Consumers are also using smart speakers for voice commerce. Of those with smart speakers in their homes in the U.S., half (49 percent) of consumers shop via smart speaker, while most (85 percent) of them still shop in stores. The study also found that smart speakers aren't just for reordering regular shopping list products but also for make first-time purchases. While 44 percent of consumers use their smart speakers for reordering, almost as many (42 percent) use them to make first-time purchases. Smart speaker growth will only continue. A quarter (25 percent) of those who don't have a smart speaker are interested in getting one.

Smart speakers have come out of nowhere. Over a two-year period, smart speakers went from fewer than 1 percent of the U.S. population having access to one to around 20 percent, according to one survey. More than a quarter (26 percent) of smart speaker owners have made at least one voice purchase and 12 percent shop by voice monthly, according to the study, comprising a survey of 1,000 U.S. adults conducted by Voicebot and Rain. That survey found that smart speakers are placed in many rooms, including the living room (46 percent), kitchen (41 percent), bedroom (37 percent), bathroom (6 percent), dining room (6 percent), garage (6 percent) and work office (3 percent). Smart speakers also are starting to replace functions once done by other devices, most notably smartphones.

Speakers Replace Smartphones

Smart home devices are starting to replace some of the things consumers have been doing with their smartphones while at home. As might be expected, devices like Amazon Alexa and Google Home are supplanting smartphones for listening to music. This may be good news for Apple, since its high-end and pricey smart speaker HomePod targets consumers looking for good sound from a smart home speaker.

However, it's not just music for which consumers are turning to their smart speakers, but almost everything else, other than for hailing a taxi, according to a survey of 1,000 U.S. smartphone owners conducted by Localytics. For listening to music, using a smart home device has replaced using a smartphone to some degree for almost all (94 percent) consumers, and a great deal for 58 percent of them. Here's the breakdown of how many consumers are using their smart home device to replace using their smartphone either somewhat or a great deal:

- 94% -- Listen to music

- 94% -- Check the weather
- 87% -- Listen to radio
- 79% -- Find out when a TV show or movie is playing
- 79% -- Listen to a short news bulletin
- 77% -- Add an item to a shopping list
- 68% -- Listen to an audiobook
- 67% -- Make a purchase
- 67% -- Listen to a podcast
- 60% -- Order food for delivery or takeout
- 58% -- Book tickets to a show, movie or event
- 41% -- Hail a taxi

The top activities where smart home devices have replaced smartphones a great deal are listening to music, checking the weather and listening to the radio. Of those who own a smart home device, the majority (67 percent) have used it two or more times for online shopping with 18 percent of them using it 11 or more times. While smartphones remain the dominant Internet-connected devices, how they're being used at home is significantly changing. Smart speakers are coming on strong. Some smart speakers also are intended to go beyond sound.

Different Assistants for Different Things

Although Amazon is currently dominating the market for digital home assistants, one of its devices doesn't look like it's a big draw for consumers. The Echo Look has four built-in LED lights, a hands-free camera, microphone and speaker. Even though the device is a bit of a step up from the mainstay Echo, the majority of consumers have little interest in it, according to a study by BI Intelligence. Most (82 percent) consumers say they are unlikely to buy it, according to the global survey of 1,900 consumers. BI Intelligence included a description of the Amazon Look and its features in the survey, so respondents were aware of the device's capabilities. More than a quarter (27 percent) of consumers say they would never buy an Amazon Look.

Likely to purchase (BI Intelligence):
- 55% -- I'm probably not going to buy it
- 27% -- I would never buy it
- 14% -- I'll buy it in the next year
- 3% -- I'll buy it as soon as I can

Even worse, the main features of the Echo Look fail to draw interest. Almost a third of consumers say they wouldn't use the device and almost one-quarter say they would not use the style feature nor the camera, the major differentiating features from an ordinary Echo.

Why unlikely to buy Echo Look (BI Intelligence):
- 32% -- I wouldn't use it
- 23% -- I'm worried about my privacy
- 23% -- I'm not interested in the style feature
- 10% -- It's too expensive
- 6% -- I doubt the style feature would work well
- 2% -- I have something like it already

The good news for Amazon is that it also markets the Echo Show, which includes a screen. This one can make video calls and do all the other things an Echo is supposed to do with Alexa. At this stage, it appears the Echo Look, as it's configured and intended, may become a niche product. No matter the features, voice assistants are spreading to every room in the house.

Parents Become Power Users

As more consumers acquire voice-activated speakers, some patterns of usage are starting to emerge. One difference is between usage by parents and non-parents. It turns out that parents have become voice-assistance power users, based on a Google study that surveyed 1,600 U.S. adults who are active users of voice-activated speakers Amazon Echo or Google Home. In every category measured, parents conducted more voice-activated tasks weekly than non-parents. Here are the tasks done with smart speakers at least weekly by parents:

71% -- Create to-do lists

70% -- Manage calendar

70% -- Check sports scores

69% -- Search for information about local places

68% -- Use a calculator, conversions, etc.

For non-parents, just over half (52 percent) have done the four first tasks at least weekly and 48 percent have done the last activity, using a calculator. Parents also are more likely to use their voice-activated speakers throughout the day. The majority (78 percent) of parents typically use their smart speakers as part of their daily routine, compared to 67 percent of non-parents. Most (76 percent) parents also use the speakers while doing other things, compared to 62 percent of non-parents. While parents are busy interacting with smart speakers in the home, so are their children -- most notably listening to music through them. Here's what parents say their children do on their smart speakers:

- 54% -- Listen to music
- 53% -- Play games, ask to hear jokes
- 43% -- Ask for information
- 35% -- Play content on TV
- 31% -- Use a calculator, conversions, etc.

Rather than being viewed as the latest IoT tech gadgetry of early adopters, parents are figuring out that smart speakers can help make them much more efficient in the course of their day.

The smart speaker is evolving to be an actual digital assistant. The reality is finally matching the marketing

Voice Assistance, Bedroom to Bathroom

At the annual CES mega-exhibition in Las Vegas in recent years, voice has been a big deal, primarily as companies announced that their respective products could be enabled by market leader Amazon Alexa. More companies announced that they were teaming with Amazon Alexa, with the Amazon voice agent integrated into their product.

A shower from Moen now comes with Alexa built in. No need to have an Amazon Echo in the bathroom, a consumer can simply speak to the shower. Bathroom fixture maker Kohler introduced Kohler Konnect, which features voice-enabled technology for the shower, bathtub, toilet, mirror, and faucets. Whirlpool introduced a smart clothes washer and added Alexa voice control. Alexa initially was wedded to Amazon's Echo line of products, but no more. The digital voice assistant is expanding into the bathroom and the laundry room in a big way. The reality is that the voice of Amazon Alexa will essentially be everywhere. No matter where they are, voice assistants will become more involved helping consumers do what they do.

Learning as They Go

Smart home voice assistants are getting easier to lean on. Amazon's Alexa has more than 20,000 'skills,' essentially apps a person connects to by speaking to Alexa, such as through Amazon's Echo. Of course, in many cases the consumer has to recall the actual name or function of the skill to execute it, as in 'Alexa, open NASA Mars' or 'Alexa, open Flight Deals.'

The device essentially shortcuts finding and opening a mobile app. Amazon's Echo Look has a camera so owners can tell Alexa to take their photo so they can check out their outfit. Alexa can do many more things, like controlling smart lights, appliances, security systems, and playing music. For at least one person in our household, the idea of actually walking over to Starbucks, waiting in line and ordering a coffee seems like a distant memory. Order history is tracked by the Starbucks app, that info is accessed via Alexa and, after confirmation, the order is placed, with Alexa saying when it will be ready.

Alexa is hardly alone in daily life assisting. Google's voice assistant, Google Home, added step-by-step recipe instructions. When searching for recipes on Google.com, a Google Home icon appears indicating that recipe can be sent to Google Home. From there, it's a step-by-step approach, as in "OK, Google, start recipe,' 'OK, Google, next step' and so on. There are other assists outside the home as well, such as 'Ok, Google, call an Uber.' Rather than providing a window to apps, Google Home opens a window to the world of Google knowledge.

Like Alexa, Google Assistant continually learns new tricks, such as transferring money. A Google Assistant feature was added so that it could be asked to pay friends back with Google Pay. It also can be used to request money from contacts, for free, using the Assistant on Android and iOS phones in the U.S. Anyone not signed up for Google Pay will be prompted as soon as the Assistant is asked to send money to a contact. Funds are transferred almost instantaneously, even if the recipient doesn't have a Google Pay account. The recipient would receive an email or text message if they already have the Google Pay app, so they then can cash out. Executing a payment would involve saying something like "Hey, Google, request $40 from Bob for the show tonight" or "Hey Google, send Debby $12 for lunch today." The payment feature is also being added to voice-activated speakers like Google Home.

Smart home assistants are still at their early stages, but rapidly evolving. Although most (76 percent) consumers have used voice commands on devices such as smartphones or TV sets, the early days of voice assistants found only 11 percent of U.S. consumers owning either an Amazon or Google voice assistant, according to GfK research. There also was a time that only 11 percent of consumers owned a smartphone. As voice become more common for home activities, it will be used through devices in addition to smart speakers.

TV Remote Voice Control

Voice control is being added to devices besides Amazon Alexa and Google Home. LG Electronics introduced ThinQ artificial intelligence and an advanced image processor in its newest high-end TVs, allowing the TV to receive hundreds of voice requests via LGs open smart platform, as well as through third-party AI services. With AI in the TV, LG TV owners can speak directly into the remote control to control the TV. However, ThinQ also can function as a smart home hub, providing access to other smart home products, such as smart lights, smart speakers, and robotic vacuums. These then could be connected to the TV via Wi-Fi or Bluetooth, giving the consumer voice control of the devices through the TV remote.

This isn't the first innovation using a remote for voice-controlling TV programming. The Amazon Prime Video remote has voice controls so that a movie can be found by speaking the title while pressing the microphone button. Voice commands on devices from Comcast Xfinity Home also have evolved, transforming the TV remote to a voice hub for the home.

LG is using natural language processing based on its own deep learning technology DeepThinQ. Consumers can verbally search for information, video or images featuring specific content, such as 'show me surfing videos' or 'show me all the movies this actress appeared in' or 'turn the TV off when this program ends.' Voice control looks to be a feature in even larger TVs from LG. LG unveiled the industry's first 8K, 88-inch OLED (organic light-emitting diode) screen at CES. The technology provides four times the resolution of panels in 4K screens. Not to be outdone, LG rival Samsung also has a strong lineup of smart things. And voice-enabled ceiling light fixtures were introduced by GE's C by GE portfolio, so consumers can speak to voice assistant through their ceiling lights.

In an attempt to simplify the spaghetti of voice assistants in the home, Boston-based Nuance launched a 'cognitive arbitrator' at CES. The AI-powered capability connects and integrates disparate virtual assistants, third-party services and content through a single interface. The cognitive arbitrator listens to voice commands and then routes them to the specialized assistant, such as Amazon Alexa or Google Home, to do the task. New and evolved types of digital voices are making their way to market while the number of things that digital voice assistants can do in the home continues to increase.

Telling the Lights to Turn On

Digital voice assistants can be used for a wide range of things. They can be used to answer questions, such as a query about the weather today and tomorrow, for commerce, such as voice ordering a coffee from Starbucks, or to control other smart home devices. Google Home and more recently Amazon's Alexa can tell whose voice is talking to it so it can respond to the right person, making the voice assistants even more personally tuned.

More than 1 in 10 U.S. consumers own an Amazon Echo or Google Home, making the percentages relatively small but the numbers high. For example, 15 million Amazon Echo devices were sold in one year alone, according to Parks Associates. Many voice assistants also are beyond a counter decoration, with an eMarketer study finding that 36 million Americans using a voice-enabled speaker at least once a month, primarily driven by millennials.

The longer-range question is what voice assistants will be used for. The leading uses of voice assistants are for things that can be executed independently, such as requesting information like weather or traffic, finding directions, streaming music or setting alerts, according to Parks Associates. It turns out that 40 percent of smart light bulb owners use Amazon Echo or Google Home to control their devices. The lights obviously can also be controlled via smartphone app, but many consumers are finding it easier to just tell the light what to do via a voice assistant. Amazon Echo and Google Home are the most used devices for controlling the majority of smart home products. It looks like much of that control may start with a simple, but smart, light bulb. Marketers have been watching this market closely, since where consumers go, marketing and advertising messages tend to be close behind.

Advertising Follows Voice

A mass of new advertising is projected to follow smart home devices. Smart speakers will be installed in more than 70 million U.S. households within five years, according to one forecast. The majority (55 percent) of homes will have at least one device installed by then, based on the forecast by Juniper

Research, with the number of smart speakers passing 175 million. Getting revenue from consumers using smart speakers is uncertain, to say the least, since most are essentially cost-free after the initial device purchase. And that's where advertising comes in. Advertising is the biggest revenue opportunity for voice assistants, according to Juniper, which forecasts ad spending to reach nearly $19 billion globally by 2022. "Voice-based interaction presents less options than other forms of advertising, meaning less adverts are possible," says research author James Moar. "Not all voice interactions are product searches, meaning advertisers will need to adjust their strategies to build a brand's voice strategy around information provision as well as sales."

This is where companies like Pandora have a distinct advantage, since much of their business already was built on screenless interactions, well positioning them for screenless advertising. Voice assistant devices across all platforms, including smartphones, tablets, PCs, speakers, connected TVs, cars, and wearables will reach 870 million in the U.S. by 2022, an increase of 95 percent over the 450 million just a few years earlier. Despite the large number of smart home assistants, most voice assistant usage will be on smartphones, with more than 5 billion in use globally within five years. Worldwide, the number of smart speaker devices with digital assistants integrated is projected to pass 250 million in use, for an annual growth rate of 50 percent. Voice is king. That also means it can move into the realm of being used as a new payment method.

Voice Commerce

Voice assistants have taken off and now it looks like voice payments are right behind. Eight percent of U.S. adults already have used some form of voice payments, which include voice commerce, such as using speech to buy via Amazon Alexa, voice-initiated person-to-person payments, and voice-controlled bill payments. These are among the findings in a study on voice payments by BI Intelligence. By 2022, 78 million people will use voice payments, almost a third of the U.S. population, according to BII estimates based on a survey of 950 members of its panel.

An obvious main driver fueling voice payments is more voice-capable hardware. For example, more than three quarters of U.S. consumers own a smartphone, and more than half own a tablet. Three quarters of iPhone owners have used Siri and well over half of Android phone owners have used a virtual assistant on their device. Another factor is the increase in the adoption of smart speaker devices like Amazon Echo and Google Home. That number is only going up, with BI Intelligence projecting the number of smart home devices to rise to 73 million in five years. This is not to say that consumers have a lot of faith in making payments by voice. Most trusted is Apple Siri followed by Amazon Alexa.

The reality is that it talks time for masses of consumers to adopt new behaviors, no matter how good the technology. For example, more consumers are adopting voice-activated devices, but not necessarily using them to their full potential. While more than a third of online shoppers own voice-activated devices, most of them don't use them for buying things. This is based on a survey of 4,000 global adult consumers who have shopped online within the last year. The survey was conducted by Episerver in Germany, Sweden, Finland, Denmark, Norway, the U.K. and U.S.

While 39 percent of consumers in those markets own voice-assisted devices like Amazon Alexa or Google Home, 60 percent never browse on them and only 27 percent make a purchase through them. However, many consumers seem willing to give new technologies a try. For example, 30 percent would be interested in trying drone delivery and 34 percent would be interested in trying virtual or augmented reality. Even more (47 percent) would be interested in smart mirrors in dressing rooms in stores, and 45 percent would be interested in using in-store tablets to search for products and sizes. The migration to using smart devices for more shopping activity is likely to increase over time.

Artificial intelligence also is aiding the move to voice payments. The ability for computers to understand speech and machine learning both are getting better over time. There are plenty of reason consumers want to use voice, with saving time at the top of the list. As in pretty much any new technological capability adoption, there are reasons that hold some people back. For example, security is an expressed concern in just about every IoT study. As more consumers adopt more voice assistant devices, more purchasing of things will grow. It is generally easier to *say* something rather than type it. It increasingly will be up to the technology to make sure it heard correctly and placed the correct order. Of course, that doesn't mean buying things from pioneer online seller Amazon will be leading the move to voice commerce.

Amazon Purchasing Through Alexa

Millions of consumers use Amazon's Alexa for wide variety of things. The voice assistant's thousands of skills, basically voice front ends to standing apps, let a consumer talk to Alexa through an Amazon Echo device to order a coffee from Starbucks, tell the device to get an Uber or have it ask Fitbit how you're doing today. However, one thing many are *not* doing is making Amazon purchases through Alexa. The majority (85 percent) of Amazon shoppers buy at least monthly on Amazon, based on a study by Branding Brand. The study comprised a survey of 1,000 U.S. adults who shop on Amazon and make the majority of purchases for their households. More than a quarter (28 percent) of consumers buy at least weekly from Amazon and 3 percent make purchases every day. Overall selling by Amazon is not an issue, but the source device is another story. Purchases are made by desktop, smartphone, tablet, and through the Amazon website and app. Trailing every device are Alexa and Amazon Dash buttons.

How people buy from Amazon (Branding Brand):

- 37% -- Desktop, by website
- 25% -- Smartphone, by app
- 23% -- Smartphone, by website
- 7% -- Table, from website
- 5% -- Tablet, from app
- 1% -- Alexa
- 0% -- Amazon Dash buttons

Driving about a third of Amazon sales are Prime membership, followed by lowest price, with three quarters of consumers saying they think Amazon generally offers the lowest prices. Despite all the activity in online and smartphone shopping, 60 percent of consumers say they would shop at an Amazon Go grocery store if one opened in their area. Amazon's Alexa will even have that to compete with, along with ingrained Amazon purchasing habits established over a number of year, most notably the one-step buying process.

However, using smart speakers to buy things is expected to take off. Even in the early days of smart speaker. Voice shopping is already a $2 billion business and projected to grow to $40 billion by 2022. Amazon is projected to dominate the home speaker market, which will grow 55 percent of U.S. homes, according to a study comprising a survey of 1,500 smart speaker owners conducted by OC&C Strategy Consultants. Three tech giants lead the virtual assistant AI space in the U.S. Amazon's Echo, Google's Home, and Microsoft's Cortana 2 percent. Apple came to the market late with its high-end HomePod smart speaker.

There are some twists in voice commerce, however:

- Only 39% of consumers trust the personalized product selection of smart speakers
- Voice purchases tended to be standalone, lower value items
- There are only 39 retailer-connected applications within the voice shopping category
- Only 44 percent of consumers believe that smart speakers offer the best value selection of products

However, Amazon still has the upper hand. A large majority (85 percent) of consumers select the products Amazon suggests. That Alexa is one smart voice retailer.

While more people start to talk to and big things from Alexa, marketers are always looking for new ways to tap into the smart speaker phenomenon.

Fooling Voice Assistants

There are plenty of innovations surrounding the Internet of Things and Burger King came up with another one. The fast food giant created a 15-second TV spot that ended with the words 'OK Google, what is the Whopper burger?' The phrase triggered the Google Home voice assistant, along with Android devices, to say the ingredients of a Whopper. However, Google was hot on the trail. A short time after word of the ad came out, Google shut down the ability of the commercial to trigger anything in the Google devices.

This isn't the first time that audio from TV triggered actions by smart devices at home. Earlier, after a little girl ordered an expensive dollhouse through Amazon Alexa, a TV broadcaster reported on the story. The broadcaster repeated on TV what the girl says, 'Alexa, order me a dollhouse,' setting off complaints from viewers all over San Diego saying their Alexa attempted to order a dollhouse for them.

A consumer can still get the information about a Whopper by asking Google Home or an Android phone, with the burger information coming from Wikipedia. If you ask Amazon Alexa, 'Alexa, what is the Whopper burger,' the response is: 'The Whopper is a hamburger product sold by the international fast food restaurant chain Burger King and its Australian Franchise Hungry Jack's.' This was believed to be the first TV commercial specifically designed to tap into connected home devices. It likely won't be the last. The other side is how the makers of smart voice assistants are dealing with this.

Alexa in the Super Bowl

While Amazon's clever Alexa Super Bowl commercial with Alexa losing her voice received widespread praise, the online giant also had to create some slick technology behind the scenes to stop devices around the world from giving everyone their local weather forecast. The commercial opens with a woman in her bathroom asking: 'Alexa, what's the weather like today?' Of course, in the commercial, Alexa has a cold and can't totally reply. The challenge was to stop the word *Alexa* from triggering Amazon Alexa devices in homes where the game was on. Amazon created acoustic fingerprinting technology that can distinguish between the ad and actual customer utterances, according to the company.

"The trick is to suppress the unintentional waking of a device while not incorrectly rejecting the millions of people engaging with Alexa every day," says Shiv Vitaladevuni, senior manager on the Alexa machine learning team in Cambridge.

When multiple Amazon Echo devices start 'waking' simultaneously from a broadcast, such as the Super Bowl commercial, similar audio is streaming to Alexa cloud services in Amazon's AWS cloud. An algorithm in Amazon's cloud detects matching audio from distinct services and stops additional devices from responding, according to Manoj Sindhwani, Amazon director for speech recognition. Amazon acknowledges that the dynamic fingerprinting isn't perfect, but up to 80 percent to 90 percent of devices do no respond to the broadcasts thanks to the dynamic creation of the fingerprints. At least Amazon thought of this before airing the spot. Despite the popularity of smart speakers and consumers seeing them in action in TV commercials, that doesn't mean everyone wants one.

Voice Assistants Not for Everyone

Voice is a major component of the Internet of Things, but not everyone is yet comfortable with voice commands. It's one thing to bring a smartphone up close and relatively quietly say "OK Google" or "Hey Siri" or even to sit in front a computer and mutter "Hey Cortana." Those are device, up-close moments for a consumer. However, voice commands are extending well beyond the personal interactions between a person and a smartphone or PC. Even more significantly, voice commands are now needed to interact with that digital assistant that is far from up close and personal.

Much like that person wearing a mobile earpiece talking loudly as they walk down the street or wait to board a plane, consumers are being retrained to speak into the air with the expectation that their commands will be heard and executed. It turns out that not everybody wants to do that. More than a third (34 percent) are not quite on board when it comes to using voice commands with Amazon's Echo smart speaker with its voice-activated personal assistant Alexa, based on a survey of 2,600 consumers conducted by BI Intelligence.

However, voice commands are coming on strong. A Stanford University study found that speech recognition was three times faster than smartphone typing. In addition, the error rate was 20 percent lower. Some people may be self-conscious about speaking commands into the air. Almost one in five consumers would use voice commands only if there was no one else around to hear them. Some found voice commands to be creepy. On the other hand, the majority say they would be comfortable using voice commands with an Echo. Here's the breakdown of consumer attitudes toward voice-activated personal assistants, when asked if they had an Amazon Echo if they would use it to answer commands like playing music or turning on the lights:

- 66% -- Yes
- 18% -- Only if there's no one around to hear it
- 9% -- I'll stick to pen and paper
- 4% -- That's so creepy

Wait till Siri, Google, and Cortana hear about this.

Dealing with Digital Voice Assistants

Businesses have to deal with smart voice in the home, since they are fundamentally changing consumer behavior. The price of smart speakers for the home will come down, driving millions more of the devices into homes. What's not to love about smart speakers? They can play music, answer questions, and even come up with lame jokes upon request. However, the real power is around the corner, and that's what businesses need to gear for.

Thanks to artificial intelligence, discussed in the previous chapter, smart speakers are going to start to live up to their name, as in becoming even smarter. Over time, they will learn the needs and desires of those who interact with them and anticipate actions in advance. Rather than sitting there awaiting a request, smart speakers will start to offer suggestions and make recommendations. Much like Amazon years ago adopted predictive modeling technology to make product suggestions based on past purchases, smart speakers will take that to the next level. And that's where businesses need to be.

With the Internet of things, brands need to consider what their customers' future needs are and how to service those needs via digital voice assistants. As most already figured out, creating "skills," essentially allowing Amazon's Alexa to tap into a company's mobile app by voice, is a basic requirement, essentially the cost of entry. The first phase of digital voice assistants is to allow access to a mobile app by verbally asking for it. This phase simply replaced opening an app on a phone. Starbucks is a good example of more deeply integrating its mobile app ordering capability. Rather than opening the Starbucks mobile app and tapping a few things, my wife now simply says to Amazon Echo: "Alexa, order me a coffee from Starbucks." That's it. There is no advertising, just service, further establishing the brand as an innovation leader.

The next phase for smart speakers is to become more of a central control point for activities both in and out of the home. As millions more smart devices, including appliances, become integrated with daily life at home, digital voice assistants are poised to act as the central control hub. Rather than reaching for phones to activate a smart home device or even search for something, consumers will simply talk to their digital voice assistants to get that done. Consumers are going to get conditioned to use their voice assistants as conduits, not only to other smart devices in the home but also to the businesses they deal with, now and in the future. The digital assistants will become the agents -- and advocates – for consumers.

Business are about to be re-aggregated by consumers through their smart home digital assistants. A voice command from a consumer may start out and sound quite simple, but it is really only the start of initiating events that can touch multiple businesses and industries. Here's a potential voice-drive scenario of the future, all through smart home speakers, named "You," for demonstration purposes.

Scenario 1:

- Event: A light bulb in the dining room burns out.
- Command: "Hey, You. My dining room light burned out"
- Action: Digital assistant recognizes it is not a smart light bulb, like those already installed in the living room and home office. Quickly does location search of what retailers are nearby. Concludes that the nearby Lowe's and Home Depot are the best bets, so checks inventory and pricing of both 60-watt and 75-watt lightbulbs in both stores, calculating that those are the two most logical choices. Checks pricing of LED and other energy-efficient lights, looking to save consumer electricity costs. Then does comparison of energy usage of the LED vs smart light, weighed against how often the consumer has used the smart lighting features of the living room and home office lights. Notes heavy usage, since all actions have come via the smart speaker. Then checks Best Buy, Home Depot, and

Lowe's inventory to see availability and pricing of smart lights. Calculates that the smart light is a better solution for the consumer. Instantly solicits bids to get best price on a smart light and receives best offer from Walmart. Amazon instantly matches price and offers next morning delivery, for free.

- Response. "All set, Chuck"
- Translation: "I ordered you a smart light, charged it to your American Express card. I gave Amazon a one-time key code to open the door for the morning delivery and set the front door camera monitor to tape the entire transaction. Facial ID set to confirm delivery agent is from Amazon.
- Business implications: Inventory and pricing readily available. Real-time bidding engines in place. All delivery options linked into inventory, pricing, and ordering. Customer purchase history linked. Everything in real time.
- Total time of interaction: One second.
- Conversation recap:
  "Hey, You. My dining room light burned out"
  "All set, Chuck"

Scenario 2:

- Event: Need to plan two-day business trip to Atlanta.
- Command: "Hey, You. I need a round-trip flight for a two-day business trip to Atlanta, leaving Tuesday."
- Action: Digital assistant checks all frequent flyer accounts to determine flyer status and availability of all Boston-Atlanta flights on Tuesday. Delta is best option, with most non-stop flights. Second best is American. Checks Google Maps for best times for

driving to airport. Identifies flights with most available seats. Evaluates last 10 business trips and notes that customer leaves on flights mid-morning. Puts out bid to Delta and Atlanta for best-priced seat. American has best price, so gives Delta one chance to match. Delta has slightly higher price but offers complimentary upgrade to first class. Delta flight booked and digital agent books aisle seats, matching past airline seating. Driving time to airport calculated and Uber contacted to advance book car at correct time. Analyzes best ridesharing rates at return time and notes that Lyft averages better pricing than Uber at that time, so reserves Lyft to pick up at airport for return home on Thursday. Last five trips Atlanta, determined that traveler stayed at Hilton Atlanta Airport, so agent books room there with same-day cancelation option. Gives American Express credit card to guarantee room. Searches for contact info of hotel manager. Sends note to manager saying "I'm Chuck Martin's assistant and wanted to let you know that he is a Diamond member and has a reservation to check in at your fine hotel on Tuesday. Would appreciate an upgraded room, if you might have availability. Many thanks. Chuck's Assistant." Checks contact list to see if any recent relationships in Atlanta, noting that consumer met with the same person twice within the last seven trips to Atlanta. An email history scan shows an 88 percent positive comments ratio between Chuck and Brian, noting suggestions of "getting together again in the future," so sends a short email to that person, saying "I'm arranging Chuck's travel, and wanted to let you know that he will be in town Tuesday for a couple of days. Not sure of his final sked yet but wanted to give you a heads up in case your schedules may allow a meet. All the best. Chuck's Assistant." Enters all travel details into Chuck's calendar.

- Response. "All set, Chuck. Uber will at your home Tuesday at 9:30 AM. Let me know if you want to see Brian McCord while you're in Atlanta."
- Translation: "I booked the best flights, got you upgraded to first class, booked your usual Hilton hotel and let Brian McCord know you would be in town in case you want to get together."
- Business implications: Frequent flyer status weighed against seat revenue, travel load anticipated that day, calculating overall value of that frequent flyer, match past flying behavior to previous fight patterns, car services ability to compete with ridesharing services, make cloud email history, Uber vs. Lyft incenting traveler for return trip.
- Total time of interaction: One second.
- Conversation recap:
  "Hey, You. I need a round-trip flight for a two-day business trip to Atlanta, leaving Tuesday."
  "All set, Chuck. Uber will at your home Tuesday at 9:30 AM. Let me know if you want to see Brian McCord while you're in Atlanta."

Smart digital assistants in the home are going to be the conduit to create voice-triggered experiences. They will evolve to become the actual agent of the consumer. This means that rather than negotiating with consumers, businesses will find them negotiating with their customers' digital assistants. Smart speaker is really somewhat of a misnomer: these are voice-activated gateways to voice experiences fueled by artificial intelligence. Some things to consider:

- **Clarify value:** Price is only one element of a transaction and any consumers can be persuaded beyond price. Determine what matters most in each particular interaction. This can be based on past behaviors of the customer.

- **Consider competitive pricing:** Factor the competitive landscape at the moment. For retail products, benchmark real time against Amazon and Walmart.

- **Match inventory:** The Internet of Things allows real-time matching of supply, demand, price, and location. Structure and adapt accordingly.

- **Act in real time:** The time for the deal is at the moment. There are no second chances. Let brand new customers try you out.

- **Think service:** The Internet of Things is about making consumers' lives more friction free. Make everything easier.

Voice-driven interactions are only going to increase with the mass proliferation of digital voice assistants. These are only one part of the smart home, which we focus on in the next chapter.

5 SMART HOMES

Living with the Machines

Smart devices in the home are going to transform businesses all the way back to the conception and creation of products and services. Consumers may start with a simple, Internet-connected device and grow from there. Research shows that consumers who install smart devices in their homes are generally quite happy with them, and the business impact mushrooms from there. Once a consumer has a smart home device, their behaviors and expectations begin to change, and that change extends to what those consumers will expect from other companies. Companies like Samsung already saw this coming, deciding to make all TVs smart or connected TVs. Same for LG and Comcast. The addition of voice commands through Internet-connected devices at home is changing how consumers interact. Rather than typing on a PC or phone to search for information, consumers are learning to ask their smart assistant for the answer. Businesses have to become part of that ecosystems, so they can be interacted with via voice.

A smart device purchase often is a thought-out buy, rather than one on impulse, although those occur as well. For example, a consumer may have seen TV commercials for Amazon Echo, so they have a sense of what the smart speaker does. In checking out Amazon's Echo line of devices, they likely find out about Google's competing Home line of smart speakers and then make their decision. At Best Buy, consumers may learn that smart lights can be controlled by a smartphone. Those with Comcast TV services were notified that smart home devices can be controlled via the Comcast remote, just by speaking to it. Amazon's remote lets Prime users speak to its remote to find shows or movies. Although they are commonly referred to as *smart homes*, they really are homes that have smart or Internet-connected devices. As a result, companies are being required to add intelligence or Internet-connectivity to their products. GE now has smart lighting ceiling fixtures, Kohler has a smart mirror, LG a smart ceiling fan, and Whirlpool has a smart clothes washer. Besides making many things easier for consumers, smart devices in the home are going to transform what those consumers come to expect from every business they deal with. This chapter intends to detail the massive scope of the smart home market.

Counting Smart Home Devices

The number of consumers buying and owning smart devices depends on which devices are considered *smart* and how the counting is done. For example, if smart televisions are included, the number of smart device owners will be relatively high, since just about any TV sold today is a smart or connected TV. Some studies include smart televisions as part of their count and others don't.

106

One study found that smart televisions already are at a 39 percent adoption rate among people with Internet connections. That study reports that 80 percent of all consumers now report owning a smart home device. The study comprised a survey of nearly 1,000 Internet-connected U.S. adults conducted by Matter Communications, commissioned by PlumChoice and the Z-Wave Alliance. A different study later pegged the number of smart home devices at 39 million total in the U.S. That study, by BI Intelligence, did not include smart TVs as part of its smart devices count. Yet another study by Parks Associates year found that 26 million U.S. broadband households own at least one smart home device. As to percentage of households, the number also varies. If connected televisions are counted as making a home 'smart,' then three quarters of broadband households have a smart device, according to a survey of 2,000 U.S. adults conducted by The Diffusion Group. Another survey of 1,000 U.S. adults conducted by PwC found that a quarter of consumers own a smart home product.

The studies overall show the hockey-stick growth trend. The most recent found that smart home devices are catching on in the U.S., with a third of consumers owning two or more smart home devices. That study, by GfK Research, found that about half (49 percent) of U.S. consumers own at least one smart home device. The majority (58 percent) say the smart home is likely to change their lives in the next few years. The study comprised a survey of 1,000 U.S. online adults. The smart home was defined as a smart house in which most things are interconnected and excluded smart TVs, smart set-top boxes and health and fitness devices.

Among new technologies, consumer cited the smart home as the most likely to impact them.

More than a quarter (27 percent) of consumers have more than three smart home devices and another 7 percent own two or three. While half of consumers have at least one smart home technology, millennial ownership even higher, 64 percent. Smart home products currently used include digital assistant devices (21 percent), smart thermostats (18 percent) and smart coffee makers (14 percent).

"For consumers today, smart home is a reality, not just tech industry or marketing jargon," says Tom Neri, commercial director for tech and durables at GfK. "Smart home devices and services are becoming part of people's everyday lives, and the advantages of having these devices synchronize and work together are very real, in particular for home entertainment and home security systems." One potential issue identified is that the majority (68 percent) of millennials expect devices to communicate with each other, which is not always the case.

No matter the specific numbers in any of the studies, the upward trend is clear. Numerous studies show various barriers to smart device adoption, most notably price and security. Over time, knowledge of the benefits of smart or Internet-connected devices will become more widespread. More significantly, as innovation, processing, and transmission speeds continue, the actual benefits will increase. The question still to be resolved is what people are willing to pay for smart home services.

Fees for Smart Homes

Consumers have a price in mind for what they consider to be a good value for a smart home. For most consumers, the minimum price seems to be about $20 a month. Half of U.S. broadband households consider $20 or more a month for a comprehensive smart home service to be a good value, according to research by Parks Associates. On the higher end, a relatively small percentage say the service would be worth more than $50 monthly. More than 26 million U.S. households own at least one smart home device, according to Parks.

Another survey by PwC found that one in four consumers own a smart home product with price being the most stated cause of hesitating to get one. Yet another study, conducted globally by Gartner, found that 10 percent of households have a connected home solution, though a bit higher in the U.S. There are smart home devices, which can be bought and set up by consumers, and then there are smart home systems, often installed and maintained by professional organizations. The Parks study at least gives an idea of the price barriers for a *complete* smart home system.

Considered good value fee: (Parks Associates):

- 23% -- $11 to $20
- 20% -- $1 to $10
- 18% -- $21 to $30
- 13% -- $41 to $50
- 12% -- $31 to 40
- 9% -- $0
- 7% -- More than $50

Of course, the perception of what a comprehensive smart home service is can be somewhat subjective. At least there's a ballpark of where – and how much -- recurring revenue may be found by businesses providing such services. The key is that there is more than one version of a smart home.

Types of Smart Homes

Not all smart home systems are alike. There are essentially two types: those that are professionally installed and those that are more do-it-yourself like. This was quite obvious at CES in Las Vegas, with companies like ADT, Brinks, and Carrier promoting home security systems that come via their installation prowess in the field while marketers from companies like UltraSync Smart Home argue that consumers want to buy and install the systems themselves. Both are right, of course, depending on the market segment. The market reality is that there's healthy growth in the professionally installed smart home market while the self-installed market continues to lag in adoption, based on a study by BI Intelligence.

Aside from voice-activated speakers like Amazon Echo or Google Home, even the most popular do-it-yourself home devices are seeing relatively sluggish sales, according to the study, which comprised a survey of 160 U.S. members of a BI Intelligence panel, a quarter of whom own at least one smart home device. By 2021, BI Intelligence projects that 14 million homes will have a professionally installed smart home solution, many provided by legacy companies like ADT.

Meanwhile, many well-known companies still are moving full steam ahead into the smart home market. For example, Apple released its self-installed smart home ecosystem Apple Home and Google launched Google Home, with some tackling the market with the intent to enhance some element of their core business. For example, Amazon can sell goods on Amazon Prime via voice ordering through its Echo product line, even though that may not be the primary use by consumers. Google Home, meanwhile, can be used to do voice searches on Google.

Echo features used at least once (Bi Intelligence)

- 85% -- Set a timer
- 82% -- Play a song

- 66% -- Read the news
- 64% -- Set an alarm
- 62% -- Check the time
- 46% -- Control smart lights
- 45% -- Add item to shopping list
- 41% -- Connect to paid music service
- 32% -- Buy something on Amazon primer
- 30% -- Control smart thermostat

Consumer technology companies are betting the smart home market will continue to gain traction. There are three key benefits companies such as Apple and Google gain from marketing smart home devices: be able to collect and analyze data on consumer usage, build customer profiles to study consumer behavior for improved ad targeting, and ability to update devices over the air, thus avoiding potential recalls. Consistent with other studies, BI Intelligence found the main hurdles to greater smart home adoption to be high prices, consumer awareness and technological fragmentation, none of which are insignificant issues. On the positive side of smart homes, once consumers get some level of a smart home, they are satisfied with it.

Consumer Sentiments in Smart Homes

When it comes to smart home technology, most consumers are aware of it, most don't have any, and almost all of those who do are quite happy with it. One in four consumers own a smart home product but there is excitement about the future of home tech in daily lives of consumers, based on a study. Most (65 percent) consumers say they are excited about the future of smart technology as part of everyday life in their home, based on an online survey of 1,000 U.S. adults in addition to in-depth focus group discussions, conducted by PwC. Of those, about a third say they are very excited about the prospects. Despite the future optimism, the smart home technology adoption rate is far from a mass market scale. For those who don't have any smart home devices, the biggest hesitations for purchasing are price, privacy and security.

Holding people back from a smart home (PwC)
- 42% -- Price
- 17% -- Privacy and security of data
- 7% -- Don't think will actually use it
- 6% -- Complexity
- 5% -- Lack of relevancy/utility

Financing may be in the cards for smart home devices, since a majority of consumers say that a payment plan would make them more likely to make a purchase. There also doesn't seem to be one primary driving force causing consumers to buy a smart home device.

Why people buy first smart home device (PwC)
- 12% -- Want better control of my home
- 10% -- Thought it would make my home safer
- 10% -- To increase convenience
- 10% -- Was affordable and wanted to try it out
- 9% -- Thought it would improve my quality of life
- 8% -- My favorite tech brand released a product
- 7% -- Thought it would help me be more productive
- 6% -- To save money on my home bills
- 5% -- Its ability to sync with other tech devices
- 3% -- Wanted to be able to track personal info
- 1% -- Thought it would boost the value of my home

The reasons are wide and varied. From a marketing standing, people at least are learning about smart home technology, since the PwC study found 81 percent of consumers are aware of it. The most positive news for marketers of smart home gadgetry is that those who have bought in, love their devices. Almost all (98 percent) consumers are satisfied with their smart home device and of those, most (74 percent) are very satisfied. And that's a statement.

Smart Homes Drive Growth

When it comes to the number of connected devices, the counts are consistently into the billions. One forecast pegs the number of connected devices already at 12 billion. That projection, by Frost and Sullivan, says the number of connected devices will grow to more than 45 billion by 2023, at an annual growth rate of 20 percent. Another forecast says the number of connected devices globally will reach 20 billion, with another 10 billion added over the next four years. One of the main drivers of growth is the smart home, according to the forecast by Strategy Analytics. By 2020, the number of connected devices will total around 50 billion, according to the forecast.

Interestingly, smart home devices will overtake smartphones by 2021 as a share of connected IoT devices. However, the rate of growth is another issue. While the Internet of Things will grow by 17 percent annually early on, the annual growth rate will decline to 9 percent by 2021, according to the research firm. For context of the scale of the Internet of Things, the personal computer, the original connected device, now represents only five percent of the total market. However, market growth is predicated on more consumers becoming aware of smart home devices and what they do.

Consumer Awareness

There are smart devices and then there are consumers who know about smart devices. The problem is, there are many more smart devices than there are people familiar with them. Most people are familiar with smartphones and smart TVs, since pretty much any phone or TV bought today is, by definition, a smart device. However, after those two items, most consumers are not familiar with connected devices, such as smart door locks and smart thermostats, based on a study. For example, fewer than half of people are familiar with smart programmable thermostats and even fewer are familiar with smart door locks, based on a survey of 10,000 U.S. adult heads of households conducted by Parks Associates. Even smart speakers are not high on the list.

Smart home device awareness (Parks Associates)

- 80% -- Smartphone
- 59% -- Smart TV
- 40% -- Smart programmable thermostat
- 39% -- Smartwatch
- 34% -- Smart speaker with personal assistant (Amazon Echo, etc.)
- 30% -- Networked security camera
- 29% -- Smart doorbells with video
- 28% -- Smart door lock

Despite this, smart home adoption rates have been growing, with more than a quarter of broadband households having at least one device that can be turned on or off using a smartphone. More telling is that only 10 percent of consumers in broadband households use personal assistants or apps to control smart devices in their home, according to Parks Associates. Those lights and thermostats still are run by physically going to the device or a switch to manually operate it. Before masses of consumers start controlling smart devices remotely, they have to become familiar with them. IoT market growth is not hampered by the technology as much as it is by the lack of knowledge about it. There is, of course, the issue of price.

Costs of Smart Home Devices

Consumers are buying smart home devices but not as many as some would like. Many tech-savvy consumers got in early over the last few years and the number of consumers who have the devices is not insignificant. There are more than 39 million smart home devices already installed in the U.S., according to a BI Intelligence study. By 2022, that number is projected to grow to 73 million. The study, comprising a survey of 900 millennials and business leaders in a U.S. panel, defines a smart home device as any standalone object found in the home that's connected to the Internet, can be either monitored or controlled remotely and has a noncompeting primary function. As a result, this includes all smart appliances, security devices like smart locks and smart energy equipment, such as networked thermostats.

Not everyone is even aware of smart home devices and what they can do, since advertising and marketing for many of the products has not yet reached significant scale. Of course, there are other reasons consumers don't buy smart home devices, most notably, cost.

Why no smart home devices (BI Intelligence)

- 32% -- Too expensive
- 21% -- Don't see a device that fits my needs
- 17% -- Didn't think would use it
- 8% -- Don't trust the technology

There are essentially two categories of smart home system: those that are professionally installed that those that are more do-it-yourself like, as previously discussed. That 'too expensive' barrier is significant. For example, the study notes that a Nest smart thermostat retails for $250 while a Honeywell normal thermostat costs $16. However, there's an increasingly large range of smart home devices, and some appeal to consumers more than others. A bigger question may be whether consumers can afford to buy any of them.

Income Impacts Devices

Consumers can purchase smart home devices for any number of reasons. Someone may want the convenience of controlling their thermostat remotely, someone else may want to be able to ask questions through smart speakers like Amazon Echo or Google Home, and others may want to use smart security cameras to see who comes and goes. However, there may be another factor that influences the purchase decision, and that's income. It turns out that, across the board, more people with higher incomes than others either own or plan to purchase smart home devices. For example, the majority of those with high incomes own or plan to buy smart home entertainment products, more than those in the middle-income levels or the lower levels, based on a survey of 15,000 U.S. internet users conducted by Global Web Index. Income levels were segmented into the top 25 percent, middle 50 percent and bottom 25 percent. No matter the smart home product, more consumers in the top income tier own or plan to purchase smart home devices than either of the other two levels. Also, in every category, more of those in the middle tier own or plan to buy a smart home device over those in the lower income tier.

Top income devices planned (Global Web Index)

- 69% -- Smart home entertainment products
- 45% -- Voice-controlled smart assistants/speakers
- 45% -- Smart home utility products
- 44% -- Smart home security products
- 38% -- Smart health devices

The number of those in the middle 50 percent tier of income level differed from those in the higher brackets based on the product.

Middle income devices planned (Global Web Index)

- 62% -- Smart home entertainment products
- 38% -- Voice-controlled smart assistants/speakers
- 35% -- Smart home utility products
- 35% -- Smart home security products
- 34% -- Smart health devices

The survey did not ask about the purchase influence of product pricing, though other studies have found that the price of smart home products is one of the key considerations in a purchase. No matter the price, it does appear that income level also is a factor. Aside from income levels, consumers who have smart devices at home are finding many different uses for them.

Connected Home Uses

Mobile technology already got most consumers connected and the Internet of Things is doing the same for their homes. A profile of connected home users is emerging, including who they are and why they connect various things. The majority (62 percent) of connected home users are male and 38 percent are female, with the highest users being between 25 and 34 years old, according to a Nielsen study on how consumers use technology to secure their homes. The study comprised a survey of 5,900 adults who either use or are interested in connected home, car, or wearable technology. Consumers are using a wide range of connected technologies in their homes.

Consumer use of smart home tech (Nielsen)

- 58% -- Home automation
- 57% -- Wireless home security
- 34% -- Smart wireless sound system, speakers
- 26% -- Connected appliances
- 20% -- Smart home assistants
- 7% -- Other connected things over Wi-Fi

In addition to using a wide range of connected technologies, consumers also are quite busy using such devices on a daily basis.

Most frequently used automation features (Nielsen)

- 70% -- Lighting control
- 68% -- Garage door controls
- 66% -- Access monitoring and control
- 62% -- Heating, cooling control
- 57% -- Audio/video control
- 56% -- Smoke detector, carbon monoxide detector
- 55% -- Electric outlets, power strips

- 50% -- Appliance controls
- 49% -- Water control

Safety and security are the big drivers for getting connected. The vast majority (92 percent) of home security system owners agree that the reason for using a home security system is peace of mind. The percentages of households with digital assistants is relatively small but the numbers are large and growing, since consumers have plenty of reasons to eventually dive in.

Non-users' connected home interest (Nielsen)

- 71% -- Wireless home security
- 64% -- Home automation
- 38% -- Connected Appliances
- 44% -- Connected wireless speakers
- 43% -- Smart home assistant

It's not only security that appeals to consumers. Interest in other connected home gadgetry ranges from smart technology that can sense when the home occupant's normal behaviors and patterns have changed, and alert loved ones, to a smart pillow that can detect when you're awake and initiate other home automation features. About half of users of connected home technologies desire a single-device connected home system and would prefer to control all aspects of their home through a single device, service or app. We're not quite there yet. The Internet of Things is still a work in progress. There also will be an increasing number of ways to connect to other smart things in a home.

Smart Security Cameras Guard Doorsteps

There are numerous reasons for consumers to install smart cameras at their homes, but the one that comes to light during the holiday season is package theft. The majority (53 percent) of consumers know people who have had packages stolen from outside their home, according to one study, comprising a survey of 1,000 U.S. adults who live in a house or townhome. The study was conducted by Wakefield Research for Comcast, which is using the survey results as an argument for its Xfinity Home indoor and outdoor camera. Almost a third (30 percent) of those surveyed have had a package stolen from outside their home, with 16 percent of those having had two or more packages taken. Smart security cameras are commonly near the top of any list of smart home devices owned or desired.

More devices are in store for consumers to install in the future, including video doorbells (20 percent), smart thermostats (18 percent), and live streaming home security cameras (18 percent). Over the holidays, the smart devices perceived as most useful would be video doorbells (37 percent), live streaming home security (35 percent), and home security cameras to record short clips (33 percent). The key is that smart cameras can have an impact on potential package thieves.

"We've seen security cameras deter thieves," says Daniel Herscovici, general manager and senior vice president, Xfinity Home. "They're less likely to enter a property, and cameras are very helpful in capturing the identity of porch pirates or other intruders." After a package theft, a video clip from a smart security camera can be emailed to the police or package delivery company.

Cameras also are getting smarter. For example, the latest Xfinity smart camera uses an artificial-intelligence-powered computer vision algorithm developed by Comcast engineers, so the system can focus on the movement, center it and zoom in to deliver a detailed view of the activity. Consumers must expect that most packages would be stolen from their front door, since that's where 79 percent of them would put a live-streaming home security camera. Most consumers expect to have packages delivered to their homes during the holiday season. Now if they just had a smart security camera to keep an eye on those packages until they get home. While security cameras are intended to be always turns one, there are times at home that some people may want all other connected technology turned off.

Pausing the Smart Home

One of the issues with connected devices is that they're generally always on. Thanks to home networks, the central hub for television, streaming movies, phones, and smart home devices, everyone in the home also is connected. However, being connected during meals at home is seen as an issue, with almost all (98 percent) parents saying that disconnecting from devices during meals is essential to improving their family's bond. Almost half (42 percent) of parents don't remember the last time their family had a device-free meal, according to the survey of 1,000 U.S. parents conducted by Wakefield Research for Comcast.

It also works both ways, with more than half (52 percent) of parents saying they have been told by their children to put their own devices away at a family meal. In the genie-is-already-out department, many parents regret letting their children have their own connected devices, with almost half of them saying that their child's obsession with their connected devices has hurt their mental well-being.

Comcast data seems to support the parental survey, noting that the *pause device* feature on its home network controlling app has been used more than five million times since launch. The feature was also highlighted in a national TV campaign.

"It's giving parents tools to better control the internet," says Matt Strauss, executive vice president of Xfinity Services for Comcast. Strauss, who has four children, also is a user of the network-pausing technology, though not everyone in a household may be in favor of their connected devices being temporarily halted. "I can just push a button and pause all devices," says Strauss. "I love it, my wife loves it, my kids hate it." All good when turned off but connected home devices can easily cause some headaches for consumers.

Support for Smart Homes

It appears that connected or smart home devices need some support. Well, at least the people who buy those connected devices might. Some of the tech support is resolved by professional technicians for free and some is not, based on a study. More than 20 percent of U.S. broadband households have a technical support subscription, according to the study by Parks Associates. These subscriptions are to get support for a range of connected devices.

Devices with support plan (Parks Associates)
1. Smartphone
2. Smartwatch
3. Laptop
4. Flat panel TV
5. Home network router

Of those who did have a problem, some of those were taken care of for free. Of those who received help from a professional technician, here's the breakdown: 49 percent resolved the problem free of charge, 38 percent resolved problem for a one-time fee, 6 percent helped resolve the problem after agreement to enroll in a support service with a recurring fee, five percent helped resolve problem as part of an extended warranty plan, 3 percent helped resolve the problem as part of a support service previously enrolled in.

What they would pay for support (Parks Associates)

- 51% -- $9.99 a month
- 49% -- $14.00 a month
- 38% -- $19.99 a month
- 34% -- $29.99 a month

There's an even greater spread for annual support fees, with half of consumers saying they would likely pay a fee of $49.99 compared to a quarter who would pay $199.99. Technical support will evolve with the market. Best Buy is the current leading provider of technical support for subscriptions for connected devices, but Amazon's decision to offer an in-home tech support is a notable treat to that, according to Parks Associates. The reality is that setting up many smart home devices is anything but simple. Nearly one fifth of smart home device owners say the process of setting up their device is inconvenient. Marketers of smart device should take note, since only a third of consumer who encounter set up problems would purchase a similar product from that brand again. In addition to using smart devices at home, they also can be used to physically let someone into that home.

Smart Door Locks

There's security relating to the Internet of Things and then there's the other side of security, relating to someone's physical home. While some consumers are moving to smart devices inside their houses, they also are migrating to connected technology that enables someone to get in – or not get in – to that same house. Despite the relatively high cost, 2 million smart door locks will be sold by 2021, according to a study by Parks Associates. Annual sales from the devices will pass $357 million within five years, with the adoption rate increasing more than 75 percent from current times. However, half of consumers view smart door locks and smart video doorbells as too expensive, according to Parks, pegging the average price of a smart door lock at $220 compared to non-connected locks for $80 to $100.

There also are the obvious concerns about the *other* security, relating to concerns that connected devices can be hacked, causing the defeat of the purpose of the lock. A third of U.S. broadband households already report problems with smart home devices, according to the study. While 20 percent of broadband households express a desire for a smart appliance, adoption is at only five percent. The issue of security, whether involving door locks or other smart home devices, is front and center in the Internet of Things. In addition to executing functions for consumers, smart home devices capture troves of behavioral data, and some of that some consumer would be willing to trade some of the data relating to them.

Sharing Smart Device Data

When it comes to sharing data from smart devices, many consumers will give it up, for a price. That price can involve simple discounts on utilities or product improvements. Roughly half of U.S. broadband households are willing to share data from their smart devices for discounts on electricity, according to research from Parks Associates. Almost as many (40 percent) would be OK with sharing data to update and improve their products.

The main communications engine driving smart home and entertainment devices, along with smartphones, is Wi-Fi, accounting for a whopping 70 percent of data used per month in U.S. broadband households, according to Harry Wang, senior director of research at Parks. "Consumer data needs will continue to increase, both in and outside the home, as between 2015 and 2020, U.S. households will acquire more than 2.3 billion connected devices," Wang says. More than three quarters of U.S. broadband households use Wi-Fi for connectivity in the home and half report using 3G or 4G services, based on the study.

Despite the prevalence of cellular services from carriers like Verizon and AT&T, Wi-Fi has become the standard smart home communication platform. This makes sense, considering the large number of smart TVs installed and the growing number of smart home devices, like thermostats and security cameras, all of which link together over Wi-Fi networks. The trading of usage data for a deal is hardly a new concept. Various studies have found that consumers would share location data for certain deals, based on their location. The key here is that not *all* people would share personal data and of those who do, it likely will not be *all* the data that gets shared. Some of that data also will come via smartphones, still the king of connected devices.

Smart Home Vs. Smartphone

Smart home devices are growing while the smartphone boom heads toward its end. In four years, annual growth of smartphones sold will have slowed from 30 percent in 2014 to a mere 4 percent, based on one study. Meanwhile, the number of connected smart devices in use will increase to somewhere around 15 billion in 2021, according to the report by Ovum.

This transformation will lead companies like Apple, Samsung, and others to seek new sources of growth in virtual reality, smart home and other remerging segments, according to Ovum.

Digital voice assistants like Amazon Echo and Google Home will account for 192 million of the four billion smart home devices in use by 2021, but their role within the home and the wider world of the augmented customer will be pivotal, according to the Ovum study. Interactive audio speakers offer a more natural way than smartphones or tablets to control smart home devices.

Even though smartphone sales will gradually slow and digital voice assistant will continue to grow, the smartphone still be a critical component of driving smart homes. By 2021, Ovum says the smartphone will have cemented its position as the most popular consumer device of all time, with more than five billion in use. Voice may be easier and more efficient, but the smartphone still will be the hub of the smart home for the foreseeable future. As consumers travel, they also are likely to come across various forms of smart devices in hotels where they stay.

Smart Home on the Road

The hotel room of the future is in the works. Marriott has teamed with Samsung and Legrand to create the next generation smart hotel room. The idea is to leverage mobile and voice technologies to personalize a hotel stay. At Marriott's IoT Guestroom Lab, a person could ask a virtual assistant for a wakeup call at a certain time, use a full-length mirror for a yoga routine, start a shower at the desired temperature pre-stored in a customer's profile, and request various housekeeping services, all via voice, according to Marriott. In addition to providing customized services for hotel guests, the project aims to create an end-to-end approach for hotel owners to deploy.

Marriott International comprises 30 hotel brands with 6,400 properties in 126 countries. These include Marriott, Ritz-Carlton and the recently acquired Starwood chain. For the project, Samsung is providing its IoT ARTIK platform and SmartThings Cloud, enabling interactive lighting and various voice activations. Legrand, which specializes in digital building technologies, also has an IoT initiative called the Eliot Program. The program is intended to serve both hotel owners as well as hotel guests, according to Karim Khalifa, senior vice president, global design, at Marriott International.

"We are seeking feedback from owners and development partners as well as our own brand leaders, who will help determine which aspects of the IoT system could work best for their brand and the brand's target customer," Khalifa told me. "At the same time, we are using the lab to gather feedback from customers, who will be the ultimate end users. Our goal is to create an intuitive experience for them so it's easy to use." The voice command approach is not yet finalized. "The current room for new build hotels uses an Alexa model to activate commands, but we have not made any final decisions about one specific product," says Khalifa.

Marriott is taking a two-pronged approach with the lab, one for existing hotels and one for new properties. "Marriott, Samsung and Legrand built two rooms in our IoT Guestroom Lab: one is a fully connected, completely immersive experience for new developments while the other is a refurbished concept that incorporates a few elements of the full IoT experience that some owners may want to include in current properties," says Khalifa. "Our goal is to create a connected solution that can be deployed throughout an entire hotel, to give guests the ability to further personalize their hotel stays." The lab is not for guests to stay at, though a Marriott exec says the company will pursue live hotel rooms for further testing later. Marriott is not alone in exploring in-room and in-hotel technology for the future.

At the Hotel and Beyond

Every industry is being impacted by the Internet of Things in one way or another and hospitality is no exception. Travelers are dealing with beacons at airports to provide more relevant location-based information as they navigate through a terminal on the way to their plane. Delta lets passengers track if their luggage made it onto the plane and Tumi has a device that tells precisely where that luggage is, anywhere in the world, via a connection to AT&T's cellular network.

Consumers arriving at major hotels also are coming face-to-face with more technology, from the time they book their room to when they enter it. MGM Resorts International has been on the high-tech road for some time and at the annual FutureM conference in Boston, one executive at the major global hotel brand discussed how the brand is tapping into tech to enhance customer engagements. Anyone who has ever visited Las Vegas likely has come across or stayed at one of MGMs destination resorts there, which include MGM Grand, Bellagio, Aria, The Mirage, Mandalay Bay, and Luxor. At a break in the event, I sat down with Beverly Jackson, vice president, social media marketing and content strategy, at MGM Resorts International, to discuss the state of technology today and going forward.

"For us, the evolution and transformation in technology is essential," says Jackson. "We deliver personalized guest experiences at scale. You can't do that without technology, which plays a central part in that, whether it's artificial intelligence or bot technology or other iterations of technology." The technology deployed is aimed at enhancing hotel experiences. "As we start to think about more of the things that we roll out, whether it's actual technology in the room, or the ability to use tablets, one-touch and voice commands, your key or your phone as the FOB to open your room door, and have your personized settings adjusted as you walk into the room, how you like your lights, how you like your water temperature, how you like the shades drawn; those are all very high-end personalized experiences that sort of feed into the space of entertainment, of hospitality. That's important, because when people feel like you know them and you can use technology to deliver those experiences, both to keep track of them and to deliver them, that means there's a greater opportunity to increase market share and revenue. Technology is at the center of almost everything we do going forward."

Like many other major global brands, MGM has to think and prepare for large scale deployments. "When you have 40,000 beds, 77,000 employees, and 27 global destinations, it becomes more and more difficult to have that one-to-one relationship that you've had with customers, so you need to use the technology to do that." Jackson notes that she is essentially one cog in a giant wheel of innovation across the MGM enterprise and, as in most successful technological innovations in organizations, the buy-in runs from the top down. "We have a lot of opportunities ahead of all of us." Smart technology also is going to be found in the *floating hotels* of cruise lines.

Smart Home at Sea

Consumers taking a future cruise are likely to run into robotics, virtual reality, digital way finders, digital personal advisors, interactive bracelets, 3D, movies and facial recognition. In a series of connected ships being introduced, Royal Caribbean's Symphony of the Seas, reportedly the world's largest cruise ship, comes with plenty of Internet of Things features. Travelers check in with a combination of facial recognition, bar codes, and beacons for faster, frictionless boarding. The Royal Caribbean cruise ship, which can carry 5,500 passengers in 2,777 staterooms, also features robot bartenders at its Bionic Bar. The ship also sports state-of-the-art wayfinding and virtual balconies.

This is part of a trend of cruise ship companies tapping into the newest connected technologies to enhance a cruise. MSC Cruises, which bills itself as the world's largest privately-owned cruise line, and the ships of Carnival Corp.'s Princess Cruises, both have been retrofitting ships to include the latest IoT technology. Some of those features include virtual reality trip planning, interactive bracelets, interactive screens, and RFID and NFC access technologies. Some passengers could also opt to skip all that, and just hang out at their balcony and remain disconnected. In addition to all the capabilities smart object in the home provide, there are also some behind-the-scenes actions intended to detect problems before they become problems.

Before Smart Appliances Fail

Whether they expect it or not, consumers buying an appliance in the future will be getting a *smart* one. And before that appliance fails, they likely will get a call suggesting that a repairman be sent out in advance of the failure. That pre-failure call is likely to be from Sears Home Services, the number one appliance service company in the U.S. At the IBM Genius of Things summit in Boston, I sat down with Mohammed Dastagir, vice president and CTO of Sears Home Services, to get the rundown on how Sears will be leveraging the artificial intelligence of IBM Watson to make sure those repair calls come in time and that the repairman of the future has the right parts on the truck for each call. "We are a business that does all the home appliance repair for all the devices we sell out of the Sears stores as well as all appliances sold within the United States," says Dastagir. "We repair, maintain and provide protection for them.

"We service pretty much all the major brands, like Whirlpool, Maytag, Samsung, etc. We also have a large portfolio business where we sell parts directly to consumers. Basically, if an appliance was, say, a Samsung and under warranty with them, Sears would likely be called to make the repair, and that's the challenging part. The service industry has not been facing this level of disruption since its inception. Essentially, we call ourselves an event-orchestrated business, which means something in your home has to fail to trigger an event. And when you call us, you're already calling from a point of emotional distress, because it's causing you that level of disruption.

"In our business, you still need that guy who shows up with a wrench and a screwdriver, hopefully on time, in the window that we've given you, between two in five, and fix it the first time and hopefully, if a part is needed, that part is on the truck. Those variables are a constant for us. The disruption we're facing today and why IoT matters to us, is the unprecedented level of connected devices that are now entering the home. That requires our technicians not to be only the guy with the screwdriver and wrench, but also the guy who is going to be able to plug into your device and run a diagnosis, a guy who can deploy a software patch, a guy who can read an error code and make some sense out of it."

The entire process of consumers purchasing an appliance and crossing their fingers that it lasts for a large number of years before having to buy a replacement are fading. Smart, Internet-connected appliances change the entire model. "The table stakes soon are going to be, when customers buy smart appliances, they don't want you to come and fix it after the event has occurred," says Dastagir. "They will expect you to know about it before that event occurs, because they are not going to accept that you're going to sit back and let that level of disruption happen in their lives. "If you have little children, and a washer and dryer that has gone out of commission, you're not going to expect that it takes five days before somebody comes out to fix it, or even three, for that matter. You're going to say 'I have a smart washer for a reason. Why didn't you know about it? Why didn't you now that something catastrophic was going to happen?'"

Those new customer expectations involve behavioral change, primarily driven by new IoT capabilities. "There is going to be a learning curve, from a consumer's standpoint, where a consumer will have to reconcile the fact that there is someone now almost managing your appliance for you. "In the future, it's going to be more that when you buy an appliance, you're going to expect that somebody is going to manage it for you, remotely. The appliance is basically going to tell us, 'I'm failing here.'" Dastagir sees a significant role for marketing in the road ahead.

"You don't go looking for a smart TV now, you expect your TV to be smart. As those things become main stream, people will have a lot more different expectations, and marketing will do their part in trying to make it main stream. That consumerizing of smart capabilities will just become table stakes." Sears Home Services handles about 20,000 jobs a day and, with millions of parts available, is challenged with having the right part on the right truck at the right time, which is where Watson comes in. The idea is that predictive maintenance can be used so that some fixes can be done over the phone and others by matching the likely needed parts and getting them onto a truck in advance of a service call. In many case, the smart appliance will self-diagnose and predict a failure in advance.

"The device will trigger a chain of events for us," says Dastagir, who notes that, at least in the short term, sensors can be placed on non-smart devices. "As long as there are nuts and bolts and gears, you'll always need that guy with the screwdriver and a wrench. The question is how informed is he going to be when he walks into your door and has in his arsenal the right parts to fix it the first time."

Monitor Behavior, Not Technology

As a starting point, businesses should acknowledge that all homes will become smart homes, to one degree or another. Some of these homes will be made smart by outside entities anywhere in the world, such as Verizon, Deutsche Telecom, Comcast, British Gas, and Asia Smart Home. In those cases, consumers turn to those suppliers to make everything in their home work together. That can sometimes be tricky, at least in the short term, as a steady stream of new, individual smart devices floods the market. Other homes will be made smart by individuals who want to set things up themselves, so they make individual device purchases and give it a go. They may look to

Amazon, Apple, or Google for devices to act as central control points. The reality is that the smart home market is complex.

A consumer's situation and demographic may determine the smart home approach. For example, an older Baby Boomer home owner may want a security system installed by ADT or Comcast and subscribe to monthly remote monitoring. Meanwhile, a Millennial renting an apartment may opt to buy a totally portable security system at Best Buy, so they can easily take it with them in a move. Their monitoring may consist of a smartphone message sent via their home network if there's an intrusion. In either case, a smart security system is added to a home.

Thanks to smartphones and Internet-connected televisions, consumers are being introduced to new capabilities, whether from remotely ordering almost anything from their phone to streaming new entertainment offerings from Netflix or Amazon Prime rather than from tradition networks. Over time, consumers will learn more about the conveniences of smart home devices. Whether desired or not, more Internet-connected devices will enter homes and impact behavior.

However, just because a device has many smart features built it, it doesn't mean everyone will use them. For example, a consumer may purchase a new LG washing machine that comes with ThinQ connectivity, a Bosch Home Connect dishwasher, or a Frigidaire Cool Connect smart air conditioner, devices that can be controlled by various voice agents, such as Amazon Alexa or Google Assistant. That's how appliances are now being made, with connectivity built in as a core component. Even with such devices in the home, many consumers still will put clothes in the washer and turn it on while there, load dishes into the dishwasher and start the cycle from the front button and turn on the air condition at the device itself. Just because a device is technologically capable of doing something doesn't mean all its features will be used. It's not about the technology, it's about the behavior. Surprisingly, after all these years, not every driver has E-ZPass.

On the other side, there are consumers who will totally embrace smart homes, which will change their expectation of all businesses they deal with. It will be assumed that any business products or services can be tapped into through digital voice assistants, like Amazon Alexa or Google Assistant, as discussed in the previous chapter. Consumers will also expect that smart devices they purchase will work together with other smart devices they have. They will expect to be able to control features in their homes from their smartphones, TV remote control, or voice assistant, without hassle. They will want outside businesses to be plug-and-play compatible with their smart home devices. The automated conveniences of smart homes will translate to expectations at work. If a consumer can easily order a product by simply saying it out loud, they will come to expect the same capabilities at work. Some things to consider:

- **Plan for a segmented market:** For some time, some consumers will continue doing things the way they have always done things, while others will dive into the full potential of smart homes. Both types of consumers may look and act the same outside of their home.

- **Track Internet-connectable vs. Internet-connected**: Monitoring sales of connected devices may provide an inaccurate picture. Watch for consumer interactions with Internet-connected devices in their homes rather than the number and types of smart devices installed there.

- **Monitor behaviors, not devices:** It's not about the technology, it's about the evolving consumer behavior, which will translate to elevated expectations from other businesses.

- **Connect with connected devices**: Make sure your products or services can be reached easily, remotely, and quickly from connected devices in the home.

- **Start small and learn**: Interact with customers through their connected devices, starting with one at a time.

- **Free up consumer time**: Consumers want to automate things to given them more time to do other things. Focus on making a consumer's life easier.

Over time, new patterns of consumer purchasing will emerge as the acquisition of more products and services becomes automated through smart home devices. Massive amounts of usage data will feed from connected appliances along with data from leisure time, entertainment devices like smart TVs. Businesses will need to tap into these data streams to keep up with the pulse of the consumer. In addition to the reality of smart homes, there are other realities creeping up on consumers, most notably virtual reality and augmented reality. These growing realities are discussed in the next chapter.

6 VIRTUAL, AUGMENTED REALITY

Merging with the Machines

Virtual reality can transport a person to a different world. Augmented reality can merge some of that digital environment with the physical world. These are really two separate, but converging, digital experiences. Virtual reality requires a headset of one form of another. There are numerous versions of relatively low-cost versions that can be used by inserting a compatible smartphone into it, which got its first big market push with Google Cardboard, literally a cardboard version of a VR headset. The more serious and immersive virtual reality requires a higher-end setup, most often from market leaders Oculus, with its Oculus Rift, and HTC with its HTC Vive, both of which require some serious computing power. Augmented reality, on the other hand, involves adding digital information to what a person sees though a smartphone camera. The data appears over what's being viewed through the camera. Virtual reality is the bigger deal in the short term and augmented reality is in the longer term, primarily because augmented reality can be used by a smartphone, which most consumers have. Eventually, virtual and augmented reality will merge into what is referred to in the industry as mixed reality. Major players in mixed reality are Magic Leap and Microsoft.

Both virtual and augmented reality have been around for many years, though not in widespread use. Early versions of virtual reality could make some people nauseous, and augmented reality had few uses, until the worldwide hit game Pokémon Go put it on the map. However, aside from games, businesses are starting to find innovative ways to use new realities in business. Virtual reality already is being used for employee training, to show destinations to potential travelers, to see houses for sale at real estate offices, and for market research. It's also being used in advertising, with a 360-degree VR version also viewable on a computer.

One study shows that 360-degree virtual reality ads perform significantly better than traditional ads. Across metrics including click-through rates, viewability, and video completion, 360-degree VR ads performed better in every dimension, according to the study by OmniVirt, which analyzed 700 million ads served. VR photos were found to perform 300 percent better than regular two-dimensional photos in click-through rates, and 360 videos caused a 46 percent lift in video completion rate compared to regular videos. When presented with an interactive 360-degree video, 86 percent of users chose to interact with the video. The study also found that most viewers of 360-degree video content stare straight ahead and look up and left more often, compared to down and right, according to OmniVirt, a VR and AR ad platform.

Coming on even strong than virtual reality is augmented reality, can be used for in-the-field instructions on how to use or repair expensive equipment. This is primarily because rather than requiring some form of headgear, augmented reality just needs a smartphone or a tablet. It also doesn't require a person to *detach* from reality, basically the physical world around them. This chapter details some of the current and potential uses of both virtual and augmented reality.

Consumer Awareness of Virtual Reality

There's virtual reality and then there's the reality relating to virtual reality. Despite all the marketing and promoting of VR headsets of various types, marketers will not get much out of VR as it exists today, according to one study. However, in the long term, virtual reality will transform marketing experiences, unlike any marketing channel that has come before, according to Forrester Research. The Forrester report, 'Virtual Reality Isn't Ready for Marketing Yet,' is based on two very large surveys of online adults in the U.S., weighted to be representative of the U.S. population. The study paints a very positive long-term picture for virtual reality while identifying the obstacles to getting there. The obstacles:

- Consumers don't get it – Some 42 percent of adults say they have never heard about virtual reality headsets and 46 percent say they don't see a use for VR in their lives.
- Device penetration is niche – Advertisers traditionally favor media that masses of consumers are already using. With virtual reality, platforms like Sony PlayStation or Google Daydream are relatively new commercially. Forrester pegs the total VR headset early market at fewer than 2 percent of online adults.
- Contents costs are high – The cost to develop VR content can range anywhere from $10,000 to well over $500,000.
- Production is complicated – Using VR content requires working with a high number of disparate

partners, whose systems typically are not integrated with each other.

- Brands' forays leave consumers wanting – Most brands testing VR start with lower-cost 360-branded VR videos, typically self-serving, generating low impact among consumers.

On the positive side, those who are interested in or currently using a virtual reality device are interested in a wide range of activities for them.

Consumer interests in virtual reality (Forrester)

- 86% -- Watching movies, TV
- 85% -- Playing video games
- 84% -- Communicating with friends or family
- 82% -- Touring virtual homes, apartments
- 81% -- Shopping for goods
- 81% -- Meeting with doctors/healthcare professionals
- 81% -- Viewing concerts
- 81% -- Working, virtual workspace
- 81% -- Communicating with co-workers
- 80% -- Participating in exercise classes
- 80% -- Taking a class at a college
- 79% -- Reading magazines
- 77% -- Putting outfits together

Based on some of the advances we saw at CES, virtual reality is being developed at scale. The market detail is if and when consumers will adopt it at the same velocity as it's created. However, there are specific VR things that appeal to consumers.

Why Consumers Buy VR Headsets

It's still not really in the mass market category, but the number of virtual reality headsets to be bought are doubling year over year. One of the main reasons is that consumers still are not very familiar with virtual reality, based on one tracking study. Fewer that one in ten households plans to purchase a virtual reality headset, according to research from Parks Associates. Gaming still leads the list of VR activities.

Expected use of VR (Parks Associates)
1. Play video games
2. Watch entertainment videos
3. Virtual tours or travel
4. Watch live events (sports, concerts, etc.)
5. Social interaction
6. Educational purposes
7. Shopping

There are some obstacles holding back VR growth. For example, fewer than a quarter of consumers are familiar with virtual reality and even fewer with specific VR headsets. "Familiarity is low, with fewer than 13 percent of consumers having experienced VR first hand," says Hunter Sappington, Parks Associates researcher. Samsung's Gear VR leads the market, with Sony's PlayStation in second place. Among U.S. consumers who bought a VR headset, 31 percent bought a Samsung VR device and 12 percent bought Sony's. Approximately 77 million households will own a virtual reality headset by 2021, according to Parks. Some in the industry are working on this, such as via demos at stores including Best Buy and GameStop.

The biggest VR hurdle is likely to come down to the value proposition. While the majority of consumers say they would like to be able to experience VR in their own homes, more than half in the Parks Associates study say they do not think the experience is worth the extra expense of buying a headset. A third of consumers also found the VR experience disorienting or uncomfortable. Virtual reality still has a few hills to get over. However, once a person gets into virtual reality, they tend to like it.

Owners Happy with VR Headsets

While most people don't have virtual reality headsets, those who do seem quite happy with them. From VR headsets that work with any smartphone to those that connect to PCs, devices bought during the holiday season are exceeding the expectations of most of the people who have them, based on a study. The study comprised a survey of 1,000 U.S. adults who once or more each week watched TV or played games on any device, conducted by Magid Associates. No matter the type of VR device, they are pleasing most consumers more than they anticipated.

Performance more than expected (Magid Associates)
- 64% -- VR headset that connects to a PC
- 63% -- Playstation VR headset
- 60% -- VR headset that works with any smartphone
- 54% -- VR headset designed for a specific smartphone

Of course, there's no way of knowing how high or low consumer expectations were to begin with. No matter, satisfaction levels of those who buy a headset are off the charts. For example, 85 percent of those who bought a headset that works with any smartphone were satisfied, as were 90 percent of those who got one designed for a specific phone. Overall, 89 percent of purchasers say they were satisfied with their purchase. While video games continue to top the list of sources of VR content, there are many other categories consumers are experiencing.

Type of VR content watched by consumers with VR headset (Magid Associates)

- 63% - -Video games
- 40% -- Short-form video
- 39% -- Movies
- 31% -- Music
- 31% -- Virtual travel
- 29% -- Television shows
- 26% -- Sports
- 19% -- Vehicle simulation
- 17% -- Art
- 14% -- Extreme sports
- 14% -- Food and cooking
- 13% -- Cars
- 13% -- Virtual training
- 12% -- Fashion
- 12% -- Educational
- 11% -- Adult entertainment
- 8% -- Esports
- 7% -- Online shopping

Two of the most significant aspects, ease of use and value provided, also were positive. Almost all users of any type of VR headset found them to be easy to use and none found them to be very difficult. More than 80 percent of users of each category of headset also found them to be a good value. Those two metrics may be good news for word-of-mouth promotion and an incentive for any marketers of virtual reality to spread the word more widely. In addition to more content being created for VR experiences, the technology behind virtual reality is also evolving.

Virtual Reality at CES

The annual CES exhibition in Las Vegas is the land of out-there innovation, as long as show-goers know where to look. The days of CES being located in one location, such as the Las Vegas Convention Center, are long gone. The show is now scattered around town, in various official show locations, including the convention center, The Venetian, Aria, Monte Carlo, Wynn Las Vegas and others. However, each year the very new things are found in what is called Eureka Park, in the basement of the Sands Hotel. The Sands is also where the CES 2018 Innovation Awards are on display (I was one of the judges for the recent CES awards).

Each year at CES, I do a deep dive into Eureka Park with Leigh Christie, director, Isobar NowLab Americas, who specializes in AR, VR, IoT, and pretty much any technology that's likely to impact the future of marketing and advertising in any way. One year, Christie introduced me to technology that was behind the very early iterations of wireless virtual reality headsets. At the next CES, they arrived. After our rapid-fire visit to countless startups, I asked Christie for some of his thoughts on the show. "Eureka park is the best place at CES for innovation," says Christie. "All the 'world's firsts' and most disruptive technology projects are based there. I was surprised by the large number of augmented reality heads-up displays and counted at least a half dozen at Eureka Park alone. Improvements are coming out fast and the race is on."

While still not mass adopted, the technology behind VR continues to advance as prices continue to decline. At one display, Christie has me try some very light, wireless gloves that provide, with a high degree of accuracy, location of objects within a VR experience and the ability to select objects and interact with them. "We are seeing improved resolutions, increased field-of-view, less chromatic aberration and more stable, inside-out tracking," says Christie. "That said, most of these AR headset companies will not survive. They are up against Magic Leap and Microsoft, not to mention HTC Vive and Oculus Rift, assuming these top-of-the-line VR systems can be converted to AR with the advent of low latency (high speed), pass-through video."

I ask Christie if he noticed any shifts in market directions this time around. "Two huge trends I noticed: hearables and markerless-AR," he says. "Hearables are basically smart headphones. This is essentially an emerging touchpoint for consumers to interact with brands. That's why it's so exciting. The same thing happened with the smartphone. And with hundreds or even thousands of devices supporting Amazon's Alexa and Google Assistant, it's not out of the question that we could be having lengthy conversations with artificially intelligent personal assistants via our hearables in the very near future. Markerless-AR is just AR, only no markers are required to get depth information and track objects. This industry is moving much faster than most people predicted. Google's ARCore, for example, only requires a single camera to function. We'll be able to track pretty much anything or everything with just a few dollars' worth of parts, plus some artificial intelligence on the computer vision's software side."

Despite all the advancements in virtual reality, the experience itself is still somewhat isolating, with a person putting on a headset and essentially detaching from the physical world to be immersed in a virtual experience. That ultimately will evolve, so that more people will participate in shared VR experiences. The more significant headsets coming further down the road will be for augmented reality. These are more of a longer-term evolution, since the technology has to get better as well overcoming the issue of creating headsets, or more accurately, glasses, that consumers feel are stylish enough to wear, as well as packing enough technology to make them useful. The other virtue of augmented reality is that it merges the physical and digital worlds.

Game Developers Favor AR

Virtual reality has long been viewed as a big deal for gaming, but that may be changing, essentially in favor of augmented reality. The number of games released on VR headsets is declining while the number coming out on AR headsets is remaining steady, according to one study. While 19 percent of developers say their current game will release on VR headsets, only 17 percent say their next one would, according to the annual study, comprising a survey of 4,000 game developers conducted by the Game Developers Conference. Meanwhile, 7 percent of developers say both their current and future games would be developed for augmented reality headsets. For VR headsets, the HTC Vive passed Oculus Rift as the most popular VR platform and it remains ahead.

Developer's interests: (Game Developers Conf.)
- 33% -- HTC Vive
- 26% -- Oculus Rift
- 20% -- Sony PlayStation
- 18% -- Microsoft HoloLens
- 11% -- Samsung Gear VR
- 10% -- Magic Leap
- 9% -- Google Daydream
- 5% -- Google Cardboard

More significantly, nearly half of developers say they are not interested in VR development. Even more significantly, almost a third of developers say they don't believe VR or AR is a long-term, sustainable business, an increase from 25 percent from the previous year. The dominant immersive reality five years out will be mobile VR and AR, according to 42 percent of developers, with 21 percent saying it will be PC or console based. A smaller number say the two approaches would be equally popular. Despite all the advancements in VR headsets, including those shown at CES, as discussed earlier, it still looks like a move to mass adoption is still some time in the future, at least for gaming. Most people do not have, need, or want a VR headset, an obvious barrier to virtual reality adoption. Augmented reality, on the other hand, has much more shorter-term potential, since all that's really needed is a phone.

Gaming also is moving in additional direction around virtual reality. For example, IBM teamed with Unity to bring the artificial intelligence of Watson to virtual and augmented reality games. The partnership allows game developers to integrate Watson cloud services into their Unity applications, such as visual recognition, speech to text and language clarification, according to an announcement by the companies.

Unity bills itself as the market leader in VR and AR for consumer use cases and its developers can now configure projects to understand speech with users and understand the intent of a user in natural language. For gaming, a player's speech could be recognized and used to trigger game events and create voice-driven interactivity in a game. For both virtual and augmented reality, the money is starting to flow.

The Money in VR, AR

It may be slow in coming, but money from virtual and augmented reality is on the way. In the short term, consumer

VR leads, but augmented reality is on track to eventually blow by it. Consumer VR will grow to $11.5 billion in 2021, according to a VR and AR revenue forecast by Artillry Intelligence. Meanwhile, consumer augmented reality is projected to grow to $15.8 billion within four years. The forecast includes devices such as headsets and smart glasses and excludes gaming consoles and smartphone-based VR. Consumer-focused VR will be hardware based in the short term, but more revenue will come from apps, games and long-form content, increasing the amount of money spent per user.

Mainstream adoption of VR is expected to be driven by price reductions by the major manufacturers Oculus, Sony, and Samsung and virtual reality is projected to continue to lead until Apple introduces it smart glasses, likely by 2020. Revenue from augmented reality, popularized by Pokémon Go, will shift to coming from hardware sales as consumer smart glasses finally arrive. Revenue from Pokémon Go reached $1 billion and Niantic, the company that makes it, received $200 million in funding to develop more games. When business applications of VR and AR added in, the revenue becomes significant. Overall global VR and AR revenue is projected to grow to $79 billion in 2021, a 160 percent annual growth rate.

The most interesting factor here is the shift coming. By 2021, with virtual reality headsets will account for only 20 percent of revenue and augmented reality 80 percent. Looking down the road for AR, Android has the advantage, with more than two billion devices compared to six hundred million iOS phones in 2021, according to Artillry. Over time, more consumers will be viewing the combination of a physical and digital world. And they likely will be *wearing* something to see that world, not looking down at their phones. In addition to gaming, consumers expect they will be using virtual reality to watch television programming down the road.

TV on Virtual Reality

Television viewing is coming to virtual reality. While VR headsets have been most notably used for gaming, many consumers around the world expect to use VR for TV and video viewing within the next few years. Almost a third of consumers say they will be watching TV via VR headset, negating the need for big screen TVs, based on a global study. The study comprised a survey of 20,0000 people in 13 countries (Brazil, Canada, China, Germany, India, Italy, Russia, South Korea, Spain, Sweden, Taiwan, the U.K. and the U.S.) who have a broadband internet connection at home and watch TV or video at least once a week. The annual study was conducted by Ericsson ConsumerLab. Many consumers expect their habits will change over the next few years, including a move to watching TV in virtual reality.

How consumers expect habits to change (Ericsson)

- 30% -- I will watch TV in virtual reality, as if I was inside the content
- 29% -- Will talk to my devices rather than using buttons or screens
- 27% -- Will get most news from social media
- 27% -- Will watch more 360-degree video content
- 25% -- Will spend more time watching video than today
- 24% -- Will get live sports from streaming services
- 20% -- Will not watch scheduled linear TV anymore
- 18% -- Will spend less time watching video content than today
- 12% -- Will not watch news on the TV anymore
- 12% -- Will watch less on-demand, since I will get lost in the variety of content
- 6% -- Will not watch on a big TV screen anymore

Of course, not everyone sees their habits changing, with almost a quarter saying they don't think they will have changed over the next five years. The big change coming is from using virtual reality as a solo experience to watching the same content together with others. More than two in five (41 percent) consumers with VR headsets already watch movies and TV programs on their devices with others and more than a third watch other video content with others.

One of the potential inhibitors to the growth of virtual reality is cost. More than half of those planning to get a virtual reality device would prefer if the headsets were cheaper. Additionally, about half of consumers think there should be more immersive content available and a third would be more interested in virtual reality if they could get a VR bundle from their TV and video provider.

The Growth of Augmented Reality

Live virtual reality, augmented reality has been around for years, in many ways waiting for technological capabilities to advance enough to make them both practical for mass consumer adoption. While Pokémon Go gave many consumers a taste of what AR could look like, with various creatures appearing in front of consumers via their smartphones, the longer-term future of AR involves head-mounted displays to bring it to a broader life. Consumer spending on AR head-mounted displays will account for more than half (53 percent) of all headset spending within five years, according to a forecast by Greenlight Insights. Spending on content and software is projected to grow 78 percent a year, reaching $15 billion by 2023.

"There are disruptions unfolding with the introduction of new handheld and head-mounted displays and exciting new markets are being created," says Clifton Dawson, CEO of Greenlight Insights. "We are expecting a faster adoption of AR headsets than what we have seen with virtual reality headsets, but optimism should be tempered as the AR ecosystem must address substantial problems on numerous base levels." Growth in the number of AR head-mounted displays is projected to be relatively low in the short term but quickly ramping up in following years.

AR head-mounted display shipments (Greenlight Insights)

- 2019 – 2 million
- 2020 – 8 million
- 2021 – 15 million
- 2022 – 24 million
- 2023 – 30 million

As can be expected, revenue is projected to move along a similar path, reaching well into the billions of dollars by 2023. One of the challenges in predicting the AR market is the number of unknowns, most notably the costs of various headsets and whether consumers will be willing to part with that much cash for an AR experience. For example, the very-long-awaited Magic Leap headset is expected to cost somewhere in the vicinity of $1,200 to $2,000. The company has raised more than $1 billion to create a wearable device and is in the process of seeking even more investments. There are lower cost alternatives, of course, such as Mira's phone-based AR for less than $100.

The median average price for AR headsets will be $950, according to Greenlight. As part of its forecast, Greenlight Insights surveyed 2,000 consumers and found that of those who want to use augmented reality, the top activities would be playing interactive games, watching live events, and navigation when driving. No matter the desired use, the mass adoption of augmented reality is still *on the way*. Besides the sheer entertainment value of virtual and augmented reality, consumer research is also being created using the technology.

VR to Measure Emotion

A virtual reality experience essentially takes a consumer into a virtual world, often quite detached from the physical world. One of the challenges of marketers has been how to understand what is happening with the consumer during that VR experience. One agency has developed a way to capture and analyze behavioral data in virtual reality. Working with the MIT Media Lab, Isobar developed a way to understand emotional states created by virtual, augmented, and mixed reality experiences. Traditional methods of user experience testing have hardly been effective. Having someone talk step-by-step during their VR experience defeats the purpose of the VR experience. Other testing, such as eye tracking, doesn't totally work because the webcam can't see most of the person's face under the VR headset. "In the traditional world, we would have to watch these people and ask questions after," Dave Meeker, vice president Isobar U.S. and global director of Isobar NowLab tells me. "Now, inside the app, all the data is captured."

Isobar's emotional tracking system uses eye tracking, electroencephalography (EEG), galvanic skin response, EKG, and facial electromyography (EMG). People using virtual reality show changes in the electrical resistance of their skin, a physiochemical response to emotions, according to Isobar. Muscle fibers contract and generate tiny electrical impulses from their faces and heatmaps follow where they go. The combo of technology lets the Isobar design team understand how a consumer is feeling during an actual VR testing session. "The issue is for us to understand emotions enough to tell when a person is open to a transaction," says Meeker. "This is about brand commerce. It's all about measuring content in 3D spaces. The goal is to measure the emotions of individuals as they go through a VR experience to validate that a campaign is eliciting the desired responses. Brands can go into the creation of VR and know it will be a good experience."

Isobar currently can test its own VR implementations with its clients, such as Wyndham. Testing is pretty straightforward, as about 15 people get wired and go through a VR experience of fewer than 10 minutes. The results can be viewed remotely, and the person viewing the results can go into the VR application to replay and see where the emotional states are and when they change. Someone has finally figured out how to monitor what people are feeling emotionally as they wander through a virtual world. In addition to researching what consumers experience during a VR or AR session, the growth in the usage of connected headsets is expected to put some pressure on those who provide the data capabilities.

VR And Wireless Networks

There may be a somewhat unintended consequence in the projected growth of virtual reality. While sales of VR headsets and revenue continue to grow, the usage of those headsets will require a substantial amount of network capability to funnel more and more content to the screens. The global market for VR headsets is projected to grow to 69 million headsets in 2022, according to International Data Corporation (IDC). The majority of the VR market is smartphone based, since most people have a phone and most don't have a separate VR headset. Longer term, the market share of virtual reality screenless viewers, such as Samsung's Gear VR, is projected to decline nine percent by 2022. Standalone head-mounted VR devices are projected to grow to 30 percent in 2022. The market share of standalone augmented reality headsets is projected to grow to 19 percent in 2022.

As VR usage grows, the data flow is about to hit mobile data networks. The data flow impact of VR will be significant, based on a study by Juniper Research. Wireless VR headsets, those that are smartphone-based and standalone, will generate more than 21,000 petabytes of streamed data in four years, according to Juniper. A petabyte is about 1,000 terabytes, or 1 million gigabytes, or 1 billion megabytes. Basically, it's quite a lot. The growth of wireless VR headset data consumption will be more than 650 percent over the next four years. While the majority of VR streamed content will come via Wi-Fi, the cellular networks also will need to provide extra capacity to handle additional data consumption, according to the study.

In the short teost VR viewing will be via smartphones, with 26 percent of the total data streamed coming from headsets tethered to PCs and consoles. This is consistent with other studies. The increasingly high resolution and refresh rates necessary for VR content means that some countries will not have the data speed capacity to handle it. Juniper defines VR as 'technology that leverages pre-determined audio and visual data from a digital source, using specific software and hardware to create an interactive and artificial environment for the user.' The coming challenge will be make sure that consumers can get and interact with all that audio and video content in very real time. This will matter to marketers, since Juniper notes that more than half of the Forbes 50 most valuable brands already are engaged in some form of VR promotion. As wireless carriers plan for a higher-speed communication future, additional uses are being found for the new realities.

VR, AR For Travel Experiences

Virtual reality can't logically replace a trip, but it sure can provide some insight into what a trip might be like. Rather than the purchase of a physical thing, travel is generally about an experience. And that's where virtual and augmented reality come in. A large majority (84 percent) of consumers globally say they would be interested in using VR or AR for travel experiences, based on a study comprising interviews of 16,000 consumers who have heard about virtual or augmented reality in Australia, Brazil, China, Germany, Japan, The Netherlands, United States, and United Kingdom. The study was conducted by research company Opinium for the payments company Worldpay.

Almost half (42 percent) of consumers believe VR and AR represent the future of tourism. Consumers will be faced with offers of virtual reality walking tours of any hotel room they might book or various cabins of an aircraft before selecting a service class or seat. It's not likely that the actual booking or paying for a trip will occur through virtual reality, since it's still easier to relay information about trip details, travel dates, passport information, and the like to a travel agent or via PC. In addition, most (57 percent) people have not ever used virtual reality, based on the Opinium survey. The study suggests that for the foreseeable future, virtual reality will primarily remain a platform for enhancing the trip planning process rather than for actual bookings.

Augmented reality has a role in travel as well. For example, in addition to Google Translate being used to instantly translate spoken words, it can use the phone's camera to translate words, such as on a sign, in real time. However, virtual reality doesn't appear to pose a threat to the travel industry. In a survey of 1,000 adults globally, the touring company Italy4Real found that more than three quarters (81 percent) of consumers globally say VR cannot replace travel and almost all (92 percent) say a virtual visit would not replace an actual visit to a destination. Virtual and augmented reality may not replace travel, but they certainly have the potential to greatly enhance a trip. The hotel industry also has taken note of virtual reality.

Virtual Reality for Hotel Tours

An IoT future is coming to hotels in the form of artificial intelligence, voice-activated, experiences and virtual reality. Consumers are willing to engage with such technologies if they feel they are in control of their experience, based on a report. The Hotel 2025 Report by Oracle is based on an audit of 250 restaurant operators, 150 hotel operators, and 700 consumers focused on their reactions to the role of technology in the guest experience over the next eight years. All kinds of technologies are on the way, ranging from facial recognition to virtual reality tours of hotels.

What hotel operators see ahead (Oracle)

- 72% -- Guest recognition by full biometrics within five years
- 72% -- AI-based systems that leverage guest preferences to make targeted dining recommendations will be mainstream by 2025
- 68% -- Virtual reality will be widespread for staff training by 2025
- 64% -- Virtual reality will be widespread for guest entertainment on property by 2025

- 63% -- Monitoring via wearable device will be in use within the next five years
- 41% -- Guests will be more likely to visit an establishment with greater frequency if they are recognized without having to give their name

There are also some potential downsides, or at least issues to give hotel and restaurant operators pause.

Potential downsides (Oracle):

- 68% -- Restaurant guests find suggestions based on digital footprint to be invasive
- 50% -- Guests say being served by a robot would not improve guest experience
- 42% -- Restaurant guests find suggestions based on health to be invasive

However, many consumers seem fine with the technology aids coming. The majority (59 percent) of hotel guests say controlling their room via voice-activated device would enhance their experience and 66 percent say virtual reality tours of hotel properties would improve their experience. Every industry will feel the effects of the Internet of Things. Even more significantly, consumers who experience IoT-driven benefits in one place will expect it in another. Any marketer not keeping up can end facing a steep hill to climb to catch up. Other industries also are looking at virtual reality to aid in their business, including real estate.

Virtual Reality in Real Estate

Businesses are starting to look virtual reality as a component of their business. One major use identified is in real estate, where one global real estate firm has jumped into virtual reality with both feet. The details of the why and how were detailed at the MediaPost IoT Marketing Forum by Anthony Hitt, CEO of Engel and Völkers, a luxury real estate company based in Germany with its North American headquarters located on Park Avenue in New York. The company has 9,000 real estate advisors in 750 locations around the world.

Virtual reality may not end up as big as augmented reality, but it is growing rapidly. Hitt says that 171 million people will be using VR hardware and software annually, making it an attractive option for the firm. "Something happened about a year ago that changed the landscape," Hitt says. "The New York Times distributed a million Google Cardboard viewers to the market. A lot of us in the virtual reality space believe that was the tipping point. That's when, all of a sudden, there were enough consumers out there for this to make sense." The real estate firm built a VR platform for a new experience and selected a Ricoh camera and then outfitted all of its North American locations with the camera and its own version of Google Cardboard viewers, Engel & Volkers branded, of course. This came to less than $1,000 per location. "For less than $1,000, we were now in virtual," Hitt says.

Real estate shoppers can go into any Engel & Völkers office, put on the viewers, and see any of the real estate listings and tour the properties via virtual reality. The real estate broker simultaneously sees what the shopper is seeing on a separate screen, so they can aid in the virtual tour. The company decided to get 90 percent of its listings on VR within the first 90 days of launch. The process involves re-photographing every listing. "We're already the first real estate brand in the world to have this virtual experience," Hitt says. "Our offices in the rest of the world are doing the same thing. "Virtual reality is something that's here now." Many creative uses are being found for virtual reality, even in research for retail.

Virtual Reality in Retail Research

Virtual reality is joining shopper marketing. A virtual supermarket was created for a major brand to measure the impact of various in-store marketing approaches. The pilot program was created by System1 Research for Hershey's chocolate to better understand how in-store signage and kiosks would impact consumer behavior relating to Hershey products. For more details, I spoke with Gabriel Aleixo, managing director, behavioral economics at System1 Research, part of System1 Group, the behavioral science and marketing company formerly known as Brainjuicer. A virtual Walmart store was created and System1 recruited 500 consumers to shop the virtual store using an HTV Vive VR headset. Several separate aisles were created in the virtual store and consumers in a hotel room went virtual shopping, one at a time, over the course of a week.

"We wanted to validate VR as a tool to replicate the in-store experience," Aleixo says. Wearing VR headsets, the shoppers roamed the aisles as System1 tracked items selected and placed in a virtual shopping cart. In the display with no merchandising used, basically the control group, 14 percent of shoppers selected a Hershey's product first. In a second display, large boards behind the display with the Hershey's brand name and logo were added. The explicit Hershey's name and logo boards actually had a negative impact on purchasing of Hershey's products, with only 10 percent of shoppers making those selections. The brand name and logo also had a negative effect on time, with the average time taken to choose any Hershey's product at 38 seconds. For both the control and still image advertising locations, the time to select a Hershey's product was only 27 seconds.

The third display included still images reinforcing the emotion of the brand. "Consumers want a fluid experience and don't want to stop," Aleixo says. "Most decisions on a shopping trip are driven by gut and intuition. People don't want to overthink those things." In the third display with the still images, Hershey products were selected first by 19 percent of shoppers.

Learned from VR shopping pilot:
- VR is a reliable means of obtaining answers to marketing questions.
- VR research and survey learning is compatible.
- VR experience needs to allow accessibility to all items, otherwise will affect results.

From the three shopping aisles, Aleixo says the researchers also learned three things:
- VR first purchase penetration is a good predictor of value sales; VR also is indicative of item price sensitivity
- VR is sensitive enough to reveal differences between pack relaunch routes, providing indication of likely impact of sales
- VR is sensitive enough to reveal uplifts in sales directly attributable to point of purchase communications

"We wanted to validate the use of VR as a tool," Aleixo says. "We believe this is the next step for shopper marketing." Virtual reality is expanding into the world of retail. In addition to research, virtual reality is also being tried for selling.

Virtual Reality for Selling Things

Virtual reality has been used for a number of applications and now commerce is moving into the picture. Nokia's marketing campaign labeled 'Healthier Together' was created to introduce its new line of digital health products. These include Nokia-branded smartwatches, connected scales, blood pressure monitors, and other consumer health devices, being shipped to stores around the world. As part of the campaign, Nokia Technologies and its agency, Brandwidth, created a virtual reality spot to immerse viewers in a real home environment, with a 'real' family, using Nokia's digital health products.

The twist is that beyond seeing the products in use by the family in the VR video, consumers could interact and make purchases directly through the VR experience, which portrays a family's theoretical journey to be healthy together. For example, the video shows the mother brushing her hair and then a digital overlay describes how she just used a smart hairbrush that can tell how healthy the person's hair is. Then there's the scale, which knows who is standing on it, and the $99 smart thermometer. These items can be added to a shopping cart by tapping a symbol at the top right of the video. A nice touch for Nokia is that the 360-VR video was shot and produced using its $40,000 Ozo+ VR camera and Creator software.

There's also a behind the scenes that shows how the spot was created and produced. How many consumers will click through the pop-up to the Nokia health site to make purchases from within a VR experience is yet to be seen. The video does, however, show via digital overlays just how much data can be captured and used in a connected household, all in real time, in front of very high-quality video.

Brands also are getting involved with virtual reality for advertising campaigns. For example, Jaguar and EasyJet both are using 360-degree virtual reality. Using the OmniVirt VR platform, Jaguar and EasyJet created the VR experience by uploading 360-degree footage onto the self-service platform, which was then launched across a network of publishers. In the Jaguar 360-degree ad, the entire inside of the car can be seen in detail by touch screen or mouse control. In addition to adding commerce capabilities inside virtual reality, the technology is being used to promote traditional movies.

Virtual Reality to Promote Movies

While Facebook may have scaled back its virtual reality activities, it doesn't mean the general public isn't getting a full dose of how the technology may look in the world of entertainment. Facebook may have closed its Oculus Story Studio as the social media giant shifted its focus away to support more external production, one of the largest movie theater chains in the U.S. created a large base where consumers could easily try virtual reality for themselves. Regal Entertainment Group teamed with AMD, Alienware, and Fox to provide a VR experience in 15 cities, inviting consumers to immerse themselves in an alien world, of sorts. The VR demos were timed around the release of the alien movie, 'Alien: Covenant.'

I dropped by one of the demonstrations of the traveling event in the lobby of the Regal Fenway Stadium 13 theater in Boston to check it out. The theater lobby features several Oculus Rift demo kiosks where viewers wait in line to check out 'Alien: Covenant In Utero,' a 360-degree VR journey from the rather scary perspective of the alien. The VR demos are free and, at the least, introduce newcomers to a high-quality VR experience. For any Alien fans, it also can get the adrenalin going before diving into the movie. Regal Crown members got access to a priority fast-track line, since the VR kiosks were prominently displayed in the lobby and could easily draw a crowd.

The interest in the virtual reality experience was high, Clint Reese from 48 Communications, the company running the VR demos, told me. The VR video, with full audio, was produced and directed by Ridley Scott, the famed Alien franchise director. The cities included on the VR tour were Knoxville, New York, San Francisco, Chicago, Philadelphia, Portland, Minneapolis, Washington DC, and Seattle. The high production quality of the virtual reality movie provided consumers a look at where VR is heading. It also may be a precursor of where movie theater experiences are heading. While virtual reality gradually evolves to provide more general consumer appeal and usage, companies are tapping the technology to help them train employees.

Virtual Reality for Employee Training

While convincing consumers to use VR headsets for shopping may not exactly be mainstream, one retailer is extending shopper use of VR to employees. Lowe's is using virtual reality to train employees in an extension of its Holoroom How To program created by Lowe's Innovation Lab. Lowe's initially launched in-store, VR-based skills training clinics in several stores. The aim of the Holoroom How To program was to teach customers basic do-it-yourself skills, such as supplies needed for a project and steps to complete one. Lowe's found that customers have about a 40 percent greater retention of steps to complete a project when using the virtual reality training. Lowe's the expanded the program with a new iteration to show associates how to use specific in-store equipment. More than 400 employees tested the VR platform and more than 90 percent reported that the VR training would help them better serve customers, according to Lowe's.

This isn't the first VR experience for retail employees. A year earlier, Walmart used virtual reality for employee training in more than 180 employee training centers. Walmart used the VR training to prepare for events such as Black Friday, operational procedures, and learning customer service. Virtual reality is also being used for shopper marketing, as previously discussed. Hershey's chocolate used a virtual Walmart store aisle to better understand how in-store signage and kiosks would impact consumer behavior relating to Hershey products.

It's not like virtual reality has moved to the head of the consumer electronics marketplace. For example, one study by Global Web Index found that fewer than one in ten Internet users in North America had a VR headset. At one Walmart trip, I saw stacks and stacks of phone-based VR headsets marked down to $1 each. Hardly flying off the shelves. While most consumers at home may not yet be attuned to the various wonders of virtual reality, some may start to learn about them at work. The coming changing dynamic is widely expected to be a shift in interest from virtual reality to augmented reality.

AR Rules in the Future

Money has been flowing into virtual reality and augmented reality, with the latter now catching the eye of investors. In a one-year period, $1.8 billion was invested in AR and VR, according to tracking numbers from Digi-Capital. However, the most recent quarter marked the start of a transition from VR-driven investments to the new mobile AR market. Venture capital and corporate investment types are now looking for mobile AR opportunities, according to Digi-Capital.

In the short term, up to 2019, Apple will have the lead in AR. However, by 2020, the situation will change, with Google taking the lead in augmented reality, surpassing Apple's AR revenue, according to the forecast. Key points from the report:

- Smart glasses remain the long-term future for AR and VR, but could take into the next decade to become a mass-consumer market

- VR's market potential has been diminished by the emergence of mobile AR as a rival platform

- Premium VR might not accelerate until second-generation, standalone VR headsets break out starting in 2019

Virtual reality is growing but cannot compare to the projected size of augmented reality. Within five years, the installed base of virtual reality could be up to 60 million users -- including those on mobile, stand-alone devices, consoles and PCs – according to Digi-Capital forecasts. Revenue would be in the range of $10 billion to $15 billion, which is no small change. However, augmented reality -- including mobile AR and smart glasses -- could reach an installed base of more than 3 billion, according to the projections. Even with an estimated 900 million mobile AR units -- including Apple ARKit, Google ARCore, Facebook Camera Effects and Snap Lens Studio being in the market, AR and VR revenue will only start to scale the following year.

Digi-Capital and others are forecasting that Apple will introduce smartphone tethered smart glasses in 2020, which could drive the smart glasses market from a few hundred thousand users last year to tens of millions of mass consumers by 2022. Meanwhile, mobile standalone virtual reality, such as Samsung Gear VR, Google Daydream View and Oculus Go, had its potential reduced by developers and phone makers shifting focus more toward augmented reality. The largest driver for augmented reality could end up being online sales.

The AR and VR market evolutions are global. For example, Starbucks in Shanghai has partnered with Alibaba for an AR-enabled roaster. While AR game revenue leads this year, non-game revenue is expected to account for more than half of AR app store revenue in four years. The largest AR ecommerce sales are projected to be from clothing, consumer electronics, automotive, health/personal care, toys, office equipment and media categories. Many consumers today use voice for interactions via devices like Amazon Echo and Google Home today. Tomorrow, they may be putting on some version of smart glasses to see the world in a different light. The big shift is a significant upgrade in the prospects for augmented reality and a major downgrade for VR. And that's the new reality.

The other significant aspect of augmented reality is that it is finally starting to get more real. Millions of consumers of all ages discovering it through Pokémon Go a while back was a start, at least for people seeing what AR actually is, even if they didn't know what to call it. Now, however, augmented reality is moving more into what consumers do day to day. For example, Lowe's introduced 'View in Your Space,' a Lowe's app feature for Android users with ARCore enabled phones that lets consumers see what products would look like in their homes before making the purchase. While browsing products in the Lowe's app, consumers tap the 'View in your Space' option. The customer then is prompted to scan their surroundings, wait a few seconds and the item appears in augmented reality.

The item then can be dragged into the desired spot, with an add-to-cart option if the consumer decides on the product. A neat feature is that the customer can walk around the product, seeing it in different perspectives, while the item remains the same size and in place. Swedish-based Ikea and other retailers also let customers view products in place via mobile AR. More companies of various categories are tapping into augmented reality. A few examples:

- Sotheby's International Realty is adding augmented reality to its international listings. The luxury realtor's Curate app enables an empty house to be shown filled with a potential buyer's choice of furniture and décor. Curate comes with a collection of AR furniture and décor sets calculated to fit in the rooms.

- Shazam teamed with Glenlivet to add a QR code to the new malt scotch whiskey The Glenlivet Code. Scanning the code leads to an AR experience featuring a hologram of Glenlivet's master distiller addressing them.

- To ramp up its AR efforts, Snap created tools for its Lens Studio to make designing AR effects simpler, which will lead to more augmented reality.

- Online marketplace eBay launched augmented reality on its app using Google's ARCore platform. The feature lets people select the proper U.S. Postal Service flat-rate box for items to be mailed.

There are many more examples and even more to come. Augmented reality finally has arrived.

The Impact on Screens

With digital assistants like Amazon Echo and Google Home coming into millions of homes, voice is becoming a common method of interacting, as discussed in an earlier chapter. The obvious question is what the role of screens will be, as voice becomes even more dominant, and that's where AR of the future comes in. I discussed some of the implications of this in the course of a wide-ranging conversation I had with Chris Neff, senior director of innovation at The Community, a global creative agency headquartered in Miami, around the future IoT technologies coming to market.

"I'm in the camp right now that screens will eventually be gone," says Neff. "I think it's an inevitability. I know I'm not the first one to say that, but, from the evidence I have, to what you can experience in thinking about the evolution of where AR will go, along with some of what Intel is working on in terms of processing, I think screens are going to be gone." At Mobile World Commerce, the $1,300 Vuzix Blade smart AR glasses were shown. The glasses use a tiny projector that can show an image in the top corner of the lenses.

"If I can get everything I need out of glasses, and eventually smart lenses too...think abouaugmentedt the evolution of the glasses," says Neff. "They're just going to continue to get smaller. The power now of the connectivity of a watch -- if I can put that information in somebody's eyes through a lens or through glasses, in terms of on the go, I won't need a phone."

I agree with Neff that the transition to homes without screens is a bit further out, especially since many families or friends watch TV together. "There are presentation screens, TV screens, and I think about it's a shared viewing experience where the screen will last the longest," says Neff. "If I'm watching TV, I could totally watch TV on one of these smart lenses or whatever. I can essentially put the TV on the wall and I can watch it. But when it's a shared viewing experience, we all need to watch it, we need to coordinate it. That a bit tricky, where it's kind of shared computing. It's a shared, kind of wireless experience. That's probably going to happen, but it's going to take longer.

"In 10 years, we're probably going to be looking at maybe 50 percent less, or 40 percent less screens than we are now and eventually, why not, if technology allows it? I don't need a screen, I'll just wear the tech," says Neff. Alexa and Google Assistant likely would be just fine with that, as if they didn't see it coming already.

One industry that ultimately could be impacted by virtual reality is television. To get into the game, CNN launched a virtual reality experience for Oculus Rift. CNN VR had been available on Android and iOS for Samsung Gear headsets and Google Daydream. Adding the Oculus Rift headset brings the VR experience to the desktop, at high resolution. The Oculus app provides an interactive experience with CNN's breaking news feed and original 360-degree stories. Viewers can select categories, such as news, for late-breaking video, or 360, for immersive 360-video from CNN journalists around the world. The CNNVR app includes a ticker scroll and social integration with CNN's Twitter accounts, so alerts also can come through the system. CNN partnered with Magnopus, a visual development company, for the VR implementation.

Augmented reality also still has uses for screens, especially in the world of beauty products. For example, L'oreal acquired ModiFace, a Canadian augmented reality and artificial intelligence company that specializes in the beauty industry. ModiFace was founded more than a decade ago and developed advanced virtual makeup technology that tracks facial features and color. The company's technology powers more than 300 custom AR apps for beauty brands, including Unilever and Allergan. It also is in smart mirrors in companies like Sephora, Coty and L'Oreal, it's new owner.

The smart mirror technology allows a customer to speak the types of colors or products they would like on their face and the mirror implements the request. ModiFace became the core of L'Oreal's digital services research and development, according to the acquisition announcement by L'Oreal. "With its world-class team, technologies and sustained track record in terms of beauty tech innovations, ModiFace will support the reinvention of the beauty experience around innovative services to help our customers discover, try and chose products and brands," stated Lubomira Rochet, chief digital officer of L'Oréal. ModiFace is remaining in Toronto as part of L'Oreal's Digital Services Factory, a network that designs and develops new digital services for the group's brands.

The New Business Realities

Even though most consumers and many businesses are not yet aware, virtual and augmented reality are no longer just for games. No doubt gaming is still a big deal for virtual reality and masses of consumers are yet to even try it, but there are plenty of business opportunities to use the technology both internally and externally. When used by a business for a specific purpose, virtual and augmented reality can be powerful.

For business in general, a way to look at the realities is that virtual reality can be most beneficial used on a controlled environment and augmented reality can be best deployed via smartphones out in the field. Augmented reality will be a bigger deal since it only requires a smartphone, which most people have access to. It's also more practical since it keeps the current, physical world in full view, rather than it being a solo adventure that can be presented via virtual reality. By 2020, some eight million augmented reality head-mounted displays will be in the market. Think Google Smart Glasses that are more fashionable and less intimidating to people facing someone wearing them.

Like many technologies of the Internet of Things, a business has to learn how the technology can be applied and what the technology can bring to their particular business. For example, a large retailer like Walmart or Target could use virtual reality to train employees for better customer interactions, or a hotel chain could create a VR experience to test how travelers would react to certain situations, as Wyndham Hotels did. A travel agency can use virtual reality in their offices so potential travelers can experience a destination or cruise, and real estate firms can use VR headsets in its offices to show properties to prospective buyers without leaving the office, as high-end, global real estate firm Engel & Volkers did.

Virtual and augmented reality can be used either internally to save money and increase productivity or externally to increase revenue or enhance customer experiences with a product or service. Because both technologies are so little known, there is still the opportunity to use the technology to create buzz around a product of service, like Regal Entertainment Group did in theater lobbies to promote a movie launch. Augmented reality can easily be added to a product, so a purchaser can aim their phone camera at a bottle of vodka or even ketchup to trigger an AR event determined by the brand. As more brands experiment with such features on their products, consumer awareness will grow. Some things to consider:

- **Attack cost centers:** Look to where augmented reality can save the business money. Payback can be quick.
- **Tap for research:** Virtual reality can be used to re-create and replace in-the-field research, such as shopper testing. Identify research underway that can be augmented or replaced with virtual reality.

- **Train in-house staff:** Virtual reality can be used for employee training, especially anything that's repetitive.

- **Add to products:** Add augmented reality to products, extending the consumer-brand experience.

- **Think globally:** Virtual reality scales easily, so it can be centrally created and globally deployed. This can assure consistent companywide messaging.

- **Consider device usage:** While most consumer don't own VR headsets, 360-degree virtual reality images can effectively be shown on a traditional PC screen, allowing the viewer to navigate around a scene.

- **Innovate:** Business uses of virtual and augmented reality are relatively new and their uses are only limited by imagination. Ask employees and customers for ideas.

7 CONNECTED CARS

Riding with the Machines

Connected vehicles are going to transform entertainment, out-of-home advertising, consumer messaging, family communication, transportation, security, privacy, delivery systems, and more. However, various vehicles, including cars, will become much more connected and technologically interactive with people in the car before individual, self-driving vehicles take off in the mass marketplace. Connectivity has been moving into vehicles for some time. One of the early iterations of basic vehicle connectivity was OnStar. With the touch of a button in the car, a driver could be in direct contact with roadside assistance, which could dispatch services based on location or even make restaurant reservations. A locked car door could be remotely unlocked by a phone call to OnStar. That type of connectivity is now widespread and commonly found in many vehicles.

Like mobile phones became an extended Internet-connection device, the same is happening with cars. In the short term, smartphones will be the conduit to the Internet while in a car, but the cars themselves are evolving to become their own mobile hub for outside connectivity. With the dramatically higher mobile speeds of 5G around the corner, more data will be available to be sent in and out of vehicles, including streaming movies and other entertainment. More cars than phones are now being added to networks, based on a study of the U.S. mobile market. The connected car segment is being dominated by AT&T with 11 straight quarters of one million or more connected car additions, according to the study by Chetan Sharma Consulting. The number of connected devices, excluding phones, passed 100 million in the U.S. and smartphone penetration stood at 93 percent. Connected vehicles was the biggest net-adds category for the year. The overall wireless market grew 18 percent while mobile data pricing dropped by 60 percent, with AT&T and Verizon on average taking the bulk of profits. Mobile data consumption is still rising with the average data consumption in the U.S. passing 6 gigabytes a month.

Cars are also getting connected to things around them. For example, more than 600 intersections in the District of Columbia have been outfitted to support the 'time-to-green' feature. Audi created a feature called Traffic Light Information so that its cars can communicate with the traffic infrastructure in certain cities and metropolitan areas, which started testing in Las Vegas some time ago. When select Audi models approach a connected traffic light, the car receives real-time signal information. When the light is red, the car's instrument cluster shows the time remaining until the signal changes to green. "Not only do V2I technologies like Traffic Light Information help to reduce driver stress, they are also essential infrastructure developments as we continue toward an automated future," says Scott Keogh, president, Audi of America. Audi and Traffic Technology Services have brought the technology to other markets, including Dallas, Houston, Palo Alto, Portland and Denver.

The automaker also introduced a vehicle-integrated toll payment system on some models so that car owners don't have to stick an additional device onto their windshields to pay for road tolls. The Integrated Toll Module (ITM) is a toll transponder built into the vehicle's rearview mirror. The technology is compatible with existing tolling agencies nationwide, which can be linked with a driver's new or current account, according to Audi. Future iterations could include integration within the vehicle's start-stop function, Green Light Optimized Speed Advisory, optimized navigation routing and other predictive services, according to the company. Audi is not alone in the traffic light department, as General Motors has been testing receiving real-time information from specially equipped traffic lights in Michigan.

Companies including Apple and Google already have staked out a position in the connected car, whose location and movement can be monitored in order to provide more relevant and timely information services to drivers. The smart home, discussed in an earlier chapter, also will intimately be linked with the connected car. This chapter focuses on what will be happening in vehicles in the future, including driving.

The Wi-Fi of Connected Cars

The concept of 'connected cars' is starting to get more real. At CES in Las Vegas a while back, General Motors executives, with the help of two cars on stage and one in the back of the room, demonstrated how they expected consumers would be using technology inside their vehicles. At that mega press event, GM announced a partnership with AT&T, so that all future Chevys would be shipped with networking technology included in the car, just as was installed in the cars on stage. At the time, GM and AT&T conceptually viewed the car as another potential mobile device on the network. Since that year, GM says it has sold more than 3 million OnStar 4G LTE-connected vehicles, more of that type of connected vehicle than any other automaker. The next year, Chevy owners used more than 4 million gigabytes of data, 200 percent more than the year before. For perspective, that means Chevrolet owners and passengers streamed the equivalent of more than 17 million hours of video. Then it gets more interesting.

Chevy owners now can get an unlimited amount of data through their car for $20 a month. This means that anyone driving or riding in a connected Chevy can tap into what effectively becomes a moving, high-speed, Wi-Fi hotspot. This model is just in time for the coming flood of additional screens in cars, which then could be linked to a car's connectivity, so that movies could be streamed in the backseat, music in the front, or a carload of kids could surf the Web. Like many mobile data plans, there's a slight caveat to what the word 'unlimited' means. The amount of data available technically is unlimited, but an OnStar advisor told me that after 22 gigabytes are used, the high speed is throttled to not-so-high speed. (For context, Cisco estimated average mobile usage to be around four gigabytes a month.) Other carmakers are likely to follow GM's lead, which would translate into a new dimension of mobile Wi-Fi connectivity, no smartphone cell plan required. This is a game-changer and opens the door to more entertainment options in coming cars.

Entertainment in Connected Cars

Along with connected cars comes in-car entertainment. More and better screens in the driver console as well as for rear-seat passengers and greater availability of in-car connectivity and Wi-Fi services will be pushing the market along, based on a study. The global in-car entertainment hardware market will reach $36 billion by 2021, according to the connected car report from Futuresource Consulting. The growth will be aided by the development and adoption of Apple CarPlay and Google/Android Auto, according to the study. This is hardly explosive growth, in relation to the dramatic increases projected in other aspects of the Internet of Things. Connected cars will grow to more than 200 million by 2020, according to Futuresource, which projects that autonomous driving will not have a significant impact through 2020. Futuresource expects autonomous vehicles to reach the consumer market by 2020, accounting for the production of 10 percent of all vehicles, but not until 2035. Of course, there are the capabilities coming inside connected cars and then there is the issue of how much of those features will actually be used by the people in those cars.

Another study suggests that many of those in-car screens will be relatively unused. While in-car browsing may be cool in concept, it's rarely used, according to a study by Drawbridge, a company that serves ads to in-car screens. Over a one-month period, the company identified that 39,000 Tesla owners used their Web browser, hardly a majority of the 150,000 total Model S and Model X cars on the road. Over a seven-day period, that figure shrinks to 6,000. When the browser is opened, it puts out requests for ads and the Drawbridge system then serves the browser with an ad relevant to the person. As a result, Drawbridge can tell when a browser is opened. The total number of ad requests for Tesla screens was one and a half million over seven days, coming to thirty-six ad requests per day per active browser. Translated, this means that a minority of owners are using the browser, but those who do are using it a lot. In terms of content requested by people inside cars, the majority accessed news content.

Content requested in cars (Drawbridge)

- 56% -- News content (40% national, 25% local, 22% international)
- 23% -- Sports-related content
- 18% -- Food and drink
- 17% -- Shopping
- 14% -- Travel
- 10% -- Real estate

The capabilities for in-car entertainment are being built, in hopes that consumer desires ad behaviors will follow. There's also the issue of the willingness of consumers to pay for new features.

Paying for Connectivity

On one side are connected cars. On the other are consumer preferences and the willingness to pay. Consumer interest in advanced automation for cars has increased since 2014 and all U.S. consumers agree that safety related technologies are useful, based on a study. The catch is that the willingness to pay for these technologies has decreased over time, with fewer than half of U.S. consumers saying they trust traditional manufacturers to bring fully autonomous vehicles to market. Fully autonomous generally means that the vehicle's technology systems have full responsibility for controlling the car. The study comprised a survey of 22,000 consumers in seventeen countries conducted by Deloitte.

Interestingly, even though the majority of American consumers don't currently use ride-hailing services like Uber and Lyft to get around, those who do see car ownership as less necessary. Younger people hailing cars are four times more likely than older consumers to question the need to own a car in the future. The good news for automakers is that the majority of U.S. consumers have a strong desire for adaptive safety features in cars, an increase of 11 percent from 2014.

Car connectedness desires (Deloitte)

- 73% -- Basic automation
- 67% -- Adaptive safety features
- 43% -- Limited self-drive
- 39% -- Fully self-drive

Then there's the issue of paying for such things. The study found that the amount U.S. consumers are willing to pay for various advanced features has declined by 30 percent since 2014. At that time, the average amount consumers were willing to pay for advanced features was $1,370. Now it's down to $925. The obvious question remaining is who will pay for all the new connected technology coming in cars. All the coming new digital activity by consumers in cars is also going to provide more new data.

Investing in Connected Cars

Autonomous cars are about data and content, and both are coming on strong. Most consumers may not be waiting in line to buy an autonomous car, but that doesn't mean a lot of money isn't flowing into the development of them. One financial boost is coming from Intel, to the tune of $250 million, according to Intel CEO Brian Krzanich, who announced the spend at the AutoMobility show in Los Angeles. However, the focus of the investment is not on actual cars, but rather on the data that will be generated from connected vehicles. "As a technologist, one of the trends I see as most disruptive to almost every industry is the enormous flood of data driven by the proliferation of smart, connected devices," Krzanich says. He estimates that every autonomous car will generate the data equivalent of about three thousand people.

Put another way, each vehicle will be generating four thousand gigabytes (four terabytes) of data a day, combining it from cameras, GPS, sonar, and radar. Key for marketers is personal data. Intel notes that there will be data that tracks how many people are in the car, music preferences of each passenger or even what stores or brands passengers prefer and, when they are near them, tee up sale items. "Wearables and other sensors inside the car can also monitor behavior, focus, emotional and biometric status to increase safety and security," says Krzanich. "Whoever has the most personal data will be able to develop and deliver the best user experience." There are three challenges around data, according to Krzanich. There's the size of data sets, the intelligence cycle needed to process the data and then, of course, security. Intel views data as the new currency of the automotive world. And now the chip giant put up $250 million in real currency to help drive that world forward. While individuals owning self-driving cars are still in the future, the idea of riding in one is another story.

Riding in Driverless Cars

The technology for self-driving vehicles is moving right along, but the question of who or what will ride inside such vehicles is still to be determined. The announcement that Waymo buying thousands of self-driving minivans for a ride hailing service is but one example of autonomous vehicles carrying people. Apple also increased its self-driving California test fleet to twenty-seven cars. However, there are other programs where self-driving vehicles are being designed to carry things rather than people. For example, the focus of Nuro, a startup by former Google engineers, is to create a vehicle to deliver things such as groceries or laundry. The vehicle is targeted for local goods transportation.

At CES, Toyota showed a concept vehicle that could carry people, but also could be used for food delivery, or even be converted essentially to self-driving food trucks. Pizza Hut already has a deal with Toyota to jointly work on pizza delivery by autonomous vehicle. At the Geneva Motor Show, another autonomous vehicle for passengers was introduced. The Renault EZ-GO is an all-electric vehicle that people can flag down via mobile app. The concept car has seats arranged in a U-shape. For Mother's Day, 1-800-Flowers.com used robots to deliver flowers, though those particular self-driving vehicles are too small to carry people, and Amazon is working on delivery of things by drone.

Ridesharing companies Uber and Lyft are the most obvious major entities to move to self-driving vehicles to replace the overhead of paid drivers. Whether the public will jump on board the driverless train is yet to be seen. A study by AAA study found that 63 percent of U.S. drivers are afraid to get into a self-driving vehicle, so there is that potential hurdle. But then again, not everyone uses Uber or Lyft for transportation. The more likely at-scale move to autonomous movement is of things. The things don't have to be convinced to get into something over which they have no control.

Autonomous Ride Sharing in Japan

Autonomous vehicles for ridesharing is a global phenomenon and not restricted to any one market. For example, Sony is launching a ride-hailing service using artificial intelligence to manage demand. The service will include six Japanese taxi companies, with 10,000 vehicles, and use Sony Payment Services, according to Sony. The service intends to use AI for the taxi dispatch service. "The services offered by the new company will be offered on a platform available to taxi operators across the country who wish to participate," states an announcement by Sony. "We plan to prepare multiple options for each business operator and aim to create a platform that allows more businesses to participate." Uber is reportedly also working to team with taxi companies in Japan. The use of artificial intelligence, the focus of an earlier chapter, is expected to aggregate and dispatch taxis more efficiently, such as anticipating when an event with many people is ending.

As another potential Uber competitor, Nissan is getting into the driverless taxi business and is field testing a robo-vehicle. In partnership with DeNA Co., Nissan launched the service called Easy Ride, according to Nissan. During the test in Yokohama, Japan, passengers can travel in vehicles equipped with autonomous driving technology along a set route. Through a mobile app, passengers can choose from a list of recommended destinations and download discount coupons from retailers and restaurants in the area. The venture aims to develop service designs for driverless environments, expanded service routes, vehicle distribution logic, pick-up and drop-off processes, and multilingual support. Passengers sit in the back seat and interact with a screen, with no driver in the vehicle.

And then there's Toyota, which formed a new company called Toyota Research Institute – Advanced Development (TRI-AD) -- to accelerate its efforts in advanced development for automated driving, the company announced. In conjunction with two other companies, Aisin Seiko and Denso Corporation, Toyota will develop fully-integrated, production-quality software for automated driving. Together, the three companies plan to invest $2.8 billion in the venture, with plans to add a staff of 1,000 employees. "Building production-quality software is a critical success factor for Toyota's automated driving program," stated Dr. James Kuffner, currently Toyota Research Institute chief technology officer, who will lead TRI-AD as its CEO. "This company's mission is to accelerate software development in a more effective and disruptive way, by augmenting the Toyota Group's capability through the hiring of world-class software engineers. We will recruit globally."

Stated objectives of the new company include creating a smooth software pipeline from research to commercialization, strengthening the collaboration within the Toyota Group and recruiting top-level engineers globally.

Fear of Riding in Self-Driving Vehicles

More consumers are starting to warm to the idea of self-driving vehicles, but most still fear riding in one. The majority (63 percent) of U.S. drivers are afraid to ride in a fully self-driving vehicle, a decrease from 78 percent a year ago, according to the annual AAA survey of 1,000 U.S. drivers. There were some demographic differences. Millennials were found to be the most trusting, with 49 percent afraid to ride in a self-driving vehicle, down from 73 percent the previous year, while the majority (68 percent) of baby boomers are afraid, down from 85 percent a year ago. More women (73 percent) than men (52 percent) are likely to be afraid to ride in a self-driving vehicle.

"Americans are starting to feel more comfortable with the idea of self-driving vehicles," says Greg Brannon, AAA automotive engineering and industry relations director.

"Compared to just a year ago, AAA found that 20 million more U.S. drivers would trust a self-driving vehicle to take them for a ride." Fewer than a third (28 percent) of drivers would trust a self-driving vehicle and 9 percent are unsure. For sharing the road with self-driving vehicles, 37 percent say it makes no difference, 13 percent would feel safer and 4 percent are unsure. While not everyone wants to ride in one, but connected cars also allow for more things to be digitally transmitted into a vehicle.

Not Buying Self-Driving Cars

While Google, Apple, Uber and most major automakers are steaming ahead to create driverless cars, the majority of consumers would not buy one even if cost was not an issue. Consumer research relating to connected cars continues to show that autonomous cars are of relatively low interest to most consumers. A study shows that the majority (57 percent) of people who currently own a connected car would not buy a self-driving car even if cost was not an issue. The study comprised a survey of 1,500 connected car drivers weighted against U.S. Census Bureau data and conducted by Solace. Those surveyed own a car with connected device features, such as Bluetooth connectivity, GPS navigation, remote door locks, Wi-Fi, backup camera/sensor or voice assistance.

However, many consumers see value in various connected features in cars. Consumers in the Solace study say the connected car alerts they would rely on are safety sensors for blind spot detection (49 percent), navigation prompts (35 percent), safety recalls (27 percent) and incoming mobile device activity (15 percent). The most valuable connected feature for driving was deemed to be real-time navigation.

When they drive, most consumers use an average of one to two applications, such as music streaming or handsfree calling.

One issue identified in the study related to data. Nearly half (48 percent) of car owners were not aware that connected cars can store personal identifiable personal information, such as home address, social security numbers and birthdays. Among the top six car brands, there was no clear leader of which had the most innovative technology features. Interestingly, 62 percent of connected car drivers believe their connected cars help them drive safer, but 40 percent won't trust their car to brake for them. The interesting marketing challenge ahead will be to change consumer attitudes toward fully autonomous vehicles. It will be interesting to see the size of *that* marketing budget.

Movies in Connected Cars

The idea of self-driving cars tends to cause some controversy, especially from those who want to keep their own hands on the wheel and want to remain in control of the driving experience. However, the *connectedness* in connected cars may, at least initially, be aimed at serving and entertaining passengers in those cars. MGM's Epix announced that its streaming video app is being integrated into the back seats of Honda's 2018 minivan. Epix says this is the first entertainment service globally to launch an app that makes its movies, original series, and other original programming available to passengers in a connected car, through a subscription to Epix, of course. "As vehicles evolve to become the ultimate mobile device, we are pleased to work with Honda to develop new entertainment experiences for second and third row passengers and pioneer this next chapter of streaming video and true TV Everywhere," says Mark Greenberg, president and CEO of Epix. This is a major step beyond the old method of using DVDs to watch movies in back seats.

Car connectivity is hardly new. Back in early 2014, at the annual CES convention in Las Vegas, General Motors and AT&T teamed to present their vision of the car of the future and how commerce could fit in. More recently, GM announced that Chevy owners now can get an unlimited amount of data through their car for $20 a month. Connected cars will grow from 30 million globally at the end of last year to more than 200 million by 2020, according to Futuresource. Futuresource expects autonomous vehicles to reach the consumer market by 2020, but not until 2035. Meanwhile, passengers in the back of Honda minivans will be streaming movies. As more screens and entertainment enters vehicles, advertising can be expected to ride along.

Advertising Inside Connected Cars

Much of the focus of connected cars or autonomous driving is on details around how the car will be networked and avoid accidents along with various aspects of reliability and security. If all that gets resolved, the marketing focus will shift to how to better serve the 'driver' in a self-driving car. An early, rudimentary version of in-car video marketing can be seen in most New York taxis, where TV-type screens in the back seat play and promote to captive passengers, until they press the *mute* or *off* button. However, some of what in-car marketing might look like in the future already is in motion in ridesharing vehicles like Uber and Lyft. This version of in-car advertising is in play in more than eleven thousand ridesharing vehicles in Los Angeles and Minneapolis, before expanding to four more markets. The difference in these TV screens -- tablets rideshare drivers install onto the backs of front seats --

is that the content involves estimated trip intent, age, and user profile of the passenger seeing the screens. The ridesharing advertising system Vugo was started by a nighttime Uber driver who worked at an ad agency by day. The system delivers relevant and targeted advertising and creates real-time deals and offers.

"We look at it as mobility media," James Bellefeuille, co-founder of Minneapolis-based Vugo Mobile Media, told me. Vugo uses what it calls its Tripintent technology to target the messaging essentially based on where the passenger likely is going. The system brings drivers additional revenue, says Bellefeuille. "It's about monetization and about content distribution." Through the Vugo screens, passengers can select a news channel to watch, for example. No matter what they watch, messaging is created and targeted for each specific trip. "Everybody hates advertising," says Bellefeuille. "This is now about empowering the passenger experience with premium content in the environment." Bellefeuille sees the day coming when cars will be driving themselves, freeing people in the vehicle from having to keep their eyes on the road all the time. "When drivers become passengers, it will be about empowering the passenger experience," he says. He also suggests that targeting advertising ultimately may subsidize being driven, opening the door to free transportation. Vugo is riding along in the back seat helping provide information and deals related to where the passenger is going. Along the way, Vugo is also gaining insights from the passengers.

There will be even more opportunity for marketers to reach consumers in vehicles, especially as more screens get added. However, there is one screen coming that advertisers are not likely to be sending traditional advertising to any time soon. this week. Screens in cars have been evolving over the years as more entertainment and car-function features get incorporated into them. Harman, a Samsung company, has been pushing forward with car connectivity and had several demonstrations I saw at CES in Las Vegas. At the back of the massive Samsung booth in the central hall was a car dashboard display with new features. In place of the traditional rear-view mirror in the center of the windshield, there was a screen, similar in shape of a mirror. The side mirrors also were gone. In place of the mirrors were three cameras and one display. Under normal driving conditions, the display would cover 150-degree side and rear views and automatically stitched images from three cameras, providing a wider view than a mirror, according to the display description. In lane-changing mode, when a turn signal is on, the side-view part of the entire display increases by 50 percent to help the driver change lanes. When the car is in reverse, the rear-view portion of the entire display increase by 50 percent. No word on details of the screen-mirror timeframe.

Advertising to Connected Drivers

While the number of connected cars is growing by the day, an ad network was launched by Allstate companies to target drivers. The catch is that rather than using the IoT technologies in cars, the network is leveraging the driving patterns of people through smartphone apps. Billed as the first telematics-based advertising network, Answer Marketplace is connecting insurance advertisers with millions of drivers via a network of publishers' apps. The idea is to use a person's driving behaviors, locations and habits -- captured via mobile device -- to provide more relevant messaging to drivers who opt in. For example, for an ad to be displayed, a user would have to be logged into the app and have completed a certain number of trips.

The network was being created by Answer Financial, an auto and home insurance agency that insures more than 3 million vehicles and homes. The IoT twist here is that the ad network is powered by Arity, a telematics and Internet of Things company founded by Allstate, which also owns Answer Financial. Arity uses data science and predictive analytics on top of its 30 billion miles of driving data and more than one virtual million active telematics connections. Developers are allowed to tap into that data, increasing the capability to understand and predict driving risk, courtesy of Arity. While the driver tracking will be done by mobile app to start, it also likely will be done by via connected vehicle down the road.

"We're device agnostic," Darren Howard, senior vice president and chief marketing officer of Answer Financial, told me. "We look at ourselves as a gateway." Answer Financial has partnerships with more than 30 insurance providers who are allowed to market through the gateway. A wealth of driving data, such as acceleration, speed, location, braking and time of day, could be captured and a driving score calculated. Suggestions also can be sent back to drivers with recommendations based on their driving patterns.

Advertisers can bid on various categories, such as miles driven, says Howard. Mobile apps already set up in the network include Life360, a leading family location and driving and safety app, and the driving reward-based Streetwise.

Initial advertisers targeted are auto insurers, but Howard says they are not placing restrictions on types of advertisers.

This means that, at least conceptually, a retailer or restaurant could bid on drivers who pass their locations a certain number of times a week, at specific times, have a propensity to stop during trips and are rated to be a certain type of driver. Other marketers, such as car dealers or car repair services, may also want to get in on the act. The connected car just got a bit more connected, without actually adding any more connections to the car itself. The connected car also has the opportunity to become a moving billboard, of sorts.

Advertising on Connected Cars

License plates are about to be turned into digital screens that display the traditional number plate information when the car is moving but convert to digital advertising when the car is parked. In a sign that the connected car is going to involve more than just Internet connectivity, a company at the auto show in Detroit introduced a digital license plate. The rPlate and information platform comes from Reviver in partnership with motor vehicle departments. The smart license plate is an IoT platform that includes DMV registration automation, hyper-local messaging, and vehicle management.

I spoke with Neville Boston, CEO and founder of Reviver, who was at the auto show to discuss some of potential of the new *plates,* which house a GPS, accelerometer, RF sensors, and storage. Initially targeted to fleets of cars, such as rental companies, the connected plates could become highly targeted mini-billboards. The rPlate is the same size as a standard license plate and has an anti-reflective screen. Advertising could be sent to license plates based on location, according to Boston. For example, a Procter and Gamble brand could be broadcast to cars all parked with a certain distance of a particular store that carried that product. "In a Home Depot parking lot, you could send ads that speak to what's in a store," Boston says.

Prototype plates already are operational in California and Reviver has approvals from state legislators in Florida and California and preliminary approval from Arizona's DMV, according to Boston. The eight-year-old company plans to launch the rPlates in Texas, Arizona, California, and Florida. Messages on the plates could dynamically change based on geolocation configuration. Already included in the plates are programming for emergency broadcasts like extreme weather warnings or Amber Alerts, as well as VIN-specific recall notifications. The plate also can automate the payment of toll road charges and parking fees. Reviver works with the local DMV with the DMV having approval of the types of advertising and messaging that could be sent through the Reviver rPlate platform. "It's always a partnership with a DMV," says Boston. "It's a public-private partnership. The rPlate is about automating really simple things."

Whether consumers will want their car to become a moving billboard, the cost of messages delivered per plate (dreading a cost-per-plate metric), and the extent of state approvals, among a host of other issues, are yet to be determined. But in true IoT fashion, anything that moves can be tracked. And license plates are constantly on the move. They're just not going to remain static. Since cars will have connectivity, they also will be able to link to other things, such as the driver's home.

Connecting Homes to Connected Cars

Connecting is the key component in the Internet of Things and consumers seem to want those connections to be pretty much wherever they are. The smartphone obviously is one of the most connected devices today and consumers look to that device as a connection for other things. It turns out that many consumers also want to link the connections in their homes with the connections in their cars, based on a study by Parks Associates. More than a quarter (27 percent) of U.S. car owners would like a feature that enables their car to communicate with

Internet-connected devices in their home. Opening a garage door or unlocking the front door from their car seems to appeal to consumers.

The reality is that *where* connections reside does not live in a vacuum. The connected car and smart home markets are growing in parallel with each other, and remote home security and controls, entertainment on-the-go, and home energy management are expanding consumer interest in connected cars, according to the report. The first preference of consumers is to have the connecting capability built into cars, followed by using a link via their smartphone. Least desirable is to use a smartphone in a car. This has potential implications for marketers, since advertising is more likely going to travel directly through car screens and speakers rather than through smartphones. Location added to the mix of targeting mobile (as in driving) consumers adds an additional twist. And how consumers pay for these connections also has to be worked out, with 61 percent of car owners preferring to bundle vehicle data with smartphone data under one billing plan.

But the linkage between home and car already is underway, with companies like Nest, ADT, Alarm.com, and Hue already creating partnerships with companies in the automotive area, according to Parks Associates. The general idea is that friction between home and away will be reduced by linking home and car, according to the report. That essentially means that messaging will have to reside in both places as well. And be connected.

Even if someone doesn't purchase a smart or connected car, they are getting more likely to come into contact with one. While manufacturers continue to add more Internet-connected features to their new and future vehicles, other entities are tapping into connectivity for their own fleets. For example, Avis tuned its mobile app to unlock car doors, flash the car headlights in a rental lot, change cars with a swipe on a smartphone. Cars and smartphones are increasingly being tied together. Intel sees the car as essentially the next smartphone, from an opportunity standpoint. Intel is not the only company looking at connecting cars to other things. BMW has created links from its cars to the owner's house, so the driver can monitor and manage systems like air conditioning remotely. And Volkswagen has teamed with smartphone maker LG to provide information both in the car or at home, the idea being that the consumers is always connected to all they own. Carmakers also are working on the longer term autonomous vehicle (AKA the self-driving car), to varying degrees. Another example is Jaguar, which is planning an all-terrain, off-road Jaguar Land Rover that has autonomous driving capabilities.

The reality is that self-driving cars hitting the roads in masses is quite a distance away, for a number of reasons, some quite obvious. In the short-term future, marketers realistically will be facing consumers who tap into information more continually and from more places, such as their cars. Rather than being around the corner, marketing to passengers who sit in cars that drive themselves is a bit down the road. Meanwhile, the actual connections themselves will have to reside in the car as well as other places.

Self-Driving Cars

Anyone overly concerned about dealing with self-driving cars while they are out and about may have plenty of time before having to worry. That doesn't mean that connected cars aren't transforming the automotive ecosystem, allowing the car and its occupants to be directly connected to the Internet, enabling automated links to other connected devices, like smartphones, tracking devices, other vehicles, and even home appliances, based on a study. There will be 15 million self-driving cars produced in 2025, according to the study 'On Track with Self-Driving Vehicles 2.0' by Juniper Research. The worldwide installed base of autonomous cars at that time is projected to be more than 22 million. By 2020, still a few years away, there will be a few thousand self-driving vehicles, according to Juniper. There are five official levels of autonomous car classifications, defined by the National Highway Traffic Safety Administration and Society of Automotive Engineers. They are:

- Level 0 – The driver completely controls the vehicle all the time.
- Level 1 – Individual vehicle controls are automated, and the driver must be ready to take control at any time. Automated systems include parking assistance with automated steering and lane-keeping assistance.
- Level 2 – Automated system controls acceleration, braking, and steering and can deactivate immediately upon takeover by the driver.
- Level 3 – Within known, limited environments, the driver can safely turn their attention from driving tasks. The car will sense when conditions require the driver to retake control and provide enough time for it. This is the eyes-off-the-road stage.
- Level 4 – Vehicle performs all functions for an entire journey with the driver not controlling the vehicle at any time. The vehicle can travel with or without a driver.

For that last one, the automotive engineers' society suggests that automated systems can control the vehicle in all but a few environments, such as severe weather. The industry group also identifies one additional final stage, where no human intervention is needed other than to set a destination and start the system with the vehicle being capable of driving to any location where it is legal to drive. Marketing and messaging to people in the car will come at the later stages, especially when watching the road is not necessary. Juniper notes that there are some dependencies for this to happen, such as reliability of technology, high accuracy maps, and software algorithms. And then these cars will need buyers.

While most self-driving car trials have a driver behind the wheel, there still are accidents, and one in 2018 involved a fatality. In a self-driving trial in Arizona, a woman crossing the street was hit by a self-driving Uber and later died. The woman had a bicycle and was crossing the street outside of a crosswalk. "Some incredibly sad news out of Arizona," stated Uber CEO Dara Khosrowshahi in a Tweet at the time. "We're thinking of the victim's family as we work with local law enforcement to understand what happened."

This is believed to be the first pedestrian fatality involving a car operating in fully autonomous mode. The car was operating in autonomous mode and there was an operator behind the wheel at the time, according to police. It is a common practice in autonomous vehicle trials to require an operator to be behind the wheel while the car is in motion. "Our hearts go out to the victim's family. We're fully cooperating with Tempe Police and local authorities as they investigate this incident," Uber said in a statement. Uber then paused self-driving operations in Phoenix, San Francisco, Toronto, and Pittsburgh.

Tempe police Sgt. Ronald Elcock says that the self-driving SUV was traveling at about 40 miles per hour when it hit the pedestrian as she stepped onto the street. He says it appears that she may have been homeless. He also says there was no impairment of the driver at the scene. The self-driving vehicle was a 2017 Volvo XC90. Police viewed the video from outside the vehicle as well as video of the driver inside the car. "Tempe police department does not determine fault in vehicular collisions," the department says in a statement to Reuters late Monday." At the press conference, Elcock says the investigation will go to the county attorney's office.

Uber has signed a deal to purchase up to 24,000 Volvo XC90 and XC60 SUVs, both of which will come with core autonomous driving technology. "We cannot speculate on the cause of the incident or what it may mean to the automated driving industry going forward," says Toyota spokesman Brian Lyons told me. "Because we feel the incident may have an emotional effect on our test drivers, Toyota Research Institute has decided to temporarily pause its Chauffeur mode testing on public roads."

Two Boston companies, Nutonomy and Optimus Ride, were asked by Boston officials to temporarily halt their tests in the Seaport area following the Arizona crash. "We have complied with the City of Boston's request to temporarily halt autonomous vehicle testing on public roads," a Nutonomy spokeswoman says. "We are working with Boston officials to ensure that our automated vehicle pilots continue to adhere to high standards of safety." It may be some time before self-driving cars are used by one individual at a time at any kind of mass scale. Meanwhile, autonomous vehicles can be used to deliver things to people.

Pizza by Driverless Vehicle

Toyota unveiled its design of a self-driving concept vehicle at CES in Las Vegas and a deal with Pizza Hut to use such a vehicle to deliver pizza was announced right after. However, there is more than that under the hood. Pizza Hut became one of the founding members of a new 'mobility services business alliance' that also includes Amazon, Mazda, Uber, and Didi, Uber's Chinese rival. Toyota's self-driving vehicle concept is called e-Palette and the intent of the global partnership is to explore the future of pizza delivery and other initiates aimed at improving mobility around the world. "In our ongoing and relentless pursuit to own and define the modern pizza experience, we are focused on technology-based solutions that enable our team members and drivers to deliver even better customer experiences," says Artie Starrs, president, Pizza Hut, U.S. "With Toyota, we are partnering with an undisputed leader in human mobility with a reputation for innovation, reliability and efficiency, as we define the pizza delivery experience of the future."

The interesting dynamic here is the combination of some major brands, such as Amazon and Uber, to collectively leverage Toyota's proprietary Mobility Services Platform to develop a suite of connected mobility advancements and create a broad-based ecosystem of hardware and software support to help a range of companies use advanced mobility tech. Toyota says it plans to start testing the e-Palette vehicle concept in several regions, including the U.S., as early as 2020. The actual last steps of the pizza delivery are likely to be handed off to yet another piece of robotics technology.

Pizza Hut delivery vehicles will be equipped with dual communication technology to capture data on driver patterns and behaviors, with plans to improve the existing driver-delivery system, including dispatching. Full deployment in the U.S. is expected a year after start. Pizza Hut previously launched voice ordering through Amazon Alexa, a pizza tracker system and the Hut Rewards loyalty program. The Toyota e-Palette could impact Pizza Hut's delivery business in the future or even serve as a mobile kitchen in parts of the world where the experience would match consumer interests, according to a joint statement from the companies.

Ford is also getting in on pizza delivery. The automaker is bringing self-driving cars to the streets of Miami and Miami Beach to deliver pizzas from Domino's. In collaboration with Miami-Dade County, Ford is testing to prove out a business model, according to Sherif Marakby, vice president, autonomous vehicles and electrification at Ford. "What we learn from this customer experience research will be applied to the design of our purpose-built self-driving vehicle that we plan to launch in 2021 to support the expansion of our service," Marakby says in the Ford announcement. The goal of the pilot program is to answers a set of questions relating to food delivery via autonomous vehicle. Marakby says the questions are:

- How will employees stock and send off a self-driving vehicle before it makes a delivery?
- At delivery, how will customers interact with the vehicle to retrieve their food or groceries?
- How far from their homes are they willing to walk to get it?
- What benefits could and should people get from a self-driving experience?

"Another way to think about it is to consider the costs of convenience," states Marakby. "Today, deliveries can be made to someone's door, though there is usually an extra charge involved. Oftentimes, drivers illegally double-park when they can't find a space, potentially causing traffic congestion for others. A self-driving vehicle won't need to be tipped and it won't park illegally." A new fleet of autonomous vehicles is already on the streets, mapping roads. Ford is also establishing its first autonomous vehicle operations terminal in Miami where it will develop vehicle management processes and house the test fleet.

Companies are starting to explore what can actually be done with self-driving vehicles, well ahead of the idea of selling them to individual consumers. Meanwhile, governments are closely monitoring the situation in relating to existing and future laws.

Regulating Connected Cars

The U.S. government is getting involved with self-driving cars, at least from a regulation standpoint. Various forms of connected cars have been coming for some time, on the road to fully autonomous vehicles. The U.S House of Representatives passed legislation that would make it easier for autonomous car makers to be exempted from normal safety standards for up to one hundred thousand cars for a one-year period while they are tested. The statute does state that "no exemption from crashworthiness standards of motor vehicle safety standards shall be granted ...until the Secretary issues the safety assessment certification." The bill, which also has to be approved by the Senate, requires that the Department of Transportation (DOT) to conduct research to determine the most cost-effective method for informing consumers about the capabilities and limitations of each highly automated vehicle as well as those that perform partial automation. After that, the DOT would start rulemaking proceedings to require manufacturers to inform consumers about such information.

The legislation defines a highly automated vehicle as one that is equipped with an automated driving system. It defines an automated driving system as the hardware and software of a vehicle that are collectively capable of performing the entire dynamic driving task on a sustained basis. The number of cars allowed to be tested starts at twenty-five thousand a year, increasing to 50,000 the second year and 100,000 in year three. The bill also includes a consumer privacy provision, requiring manufacturers to provide a written privacy plan regarding the collection, use, sharing and storing of information about vehicle owners or occupants collected by an automated vehicle.

With most major automakers along with Google, Uber, Apple, and others working on autonomous vehicles, the aim of the legislation is to speed along the deployment of self-driving cars. The new law would standardize some rules nationally rather than the state-by-state testing approaches at the moment. At least every entity would have the same rules. And any crashes would have to be reported to the federal government, whether or not they involve an insurance claim. In addition to regulations, much of the future focus is on security and creating fail-safe systems.

Hacking Connected Cars

Internet-connected cars may still have some bugs to be worked out. Researchers from a Chinese security company say they remotely tapped into the systems of a Tesla Model S and turned lights on and off, moved seats, opened the sunroof, and even shut out the driver from entering the car's system. In a blog post by Tencent's Keen Security Labs, researchers say they discovered multiple security vulnerabilities and implemented remote control of a Tesla Model S in both Parking and Driving mode. They say the car was unmodified and had the latest Tesla technology installed.

The researchers say they reported the results and technical details to Tesla, which they say was confirmed by the Tesla Product Security Team. Tesla and Keen Security Lab say it coordinated with Tesla to fix the issues, based on the blog post. In a video accompanying the researchers' blog post, the windshield wipers were remotely activated while the car was being driven. In addition, the car was remotely braked (rather abruptly, based on the video), and the trunk was opened while the car was being driven. Tesla issued and over-the-air security patch for its cars to resolve the issues, according to a statement Tesla issued. Security will remain an ongoing issue, especially as more and more technology enters vehicles.

The Technology Behind Connected Cars

At CES, plenty of connected car concepts were on display. At the mega-Samsung booth, the tech vendor, with an assist from Harman, which it bought for $8 billion some time back, a concept car was shown with the dashboard of the future, including a screen that uses cameras to replace all the rear-view mirrors. I spoke with an executive at the company in Israel that provides the complex *technological plumbing* behind all of that. "The connected car is a concept that has gained a lot of momentum in the last few years, especially with respect to the future of autonomous vehicles," says Micha Risling, senior vice president of marketing and head of the automotive business unit at Valens Automotive, a company that provides advanced automotive semiconductor technology. Valens works with companies including Samsung and Qualcomm.

"The car is becoming a data center on wheels, which automatically means that connectivity inside the vehicle is as important as the connectivity to the outside," Risling says. "The existing technologies or solutions are simply not capable of addressing the requirements of this new data center kind of approach. "The huge revolution is not just limited to autonomous, it's also infotainment, because people will have more spare time while they're driving or not driving, and they will expect the carmakers to offer them more displays, more cameras, more sensors, and all of those devices require more connectivity."

At the CES demo, Valens provided the connectivity that allowed the in-car displays to be connected to a centralized computing device. "Wiring in general is the third heaviest element in the car today," says Risling. "We refer to this as the elephant in the car. The way we see it, it's like trying to take an elephant and squeezing it into a small car. This is the issue of connectivity in the car." Risling also noted that all those working on smart or connected cars have one feature that is key. There is one issue or requirement that no one is able or willing to compromise on, and that is safety," says Risling. "Safety is becoming even more important, simply because we're starting to deal with autonomous vehicles, and, unless you do it right, there is a lot of risk associated with that. "All the carmakers will have some level of autonomous vehicles in the near future, and this will come together with better infotainment and better entertainment. Everyone understands that this is the future." One ride-sharing service has faith that the security issues will be resolved and that the self-driving fleet will arrive.

Driverless Ride Hailing Service

More vehicles will be driving themselves -- but many of them will not be the single-passenger type. The early bets in the world of autonomous vehicles are turning out to be vehicles that carry multiple people or many things. Worldwide revenue from sales of autonomous trucks and buses will grow from $87 million last year to $35 billion in four years, according to a forecast by Tractica. "The potential for autonomous trucks and buses is huge and market growth is accelerating, with news of successful pilot projects coming at an increasing pace," says Manoj Sahi, Tractica research analyst. "Considering the next two to three years as a make or break time, several prominent companies are prioritizing investment for large-scale development."

At CES, Toyota unveiled its autonomous e-Palette concept vehicle -- and it is also designed as a ride-sharing vehicle for multiple passengers as well as being able to be customized as a delivery vehicle. At the time, the automaker also announced a deal with Pizza Hut to jointly develop a self-driving pizza delivery vehicle. Meanwhile, the testing of self-driving cars continues. For example, Waymo ordered thousands of hybrid minivans for its ride-hailing service in Phoenix.

That pilot may actually become more real, since the state department of transportation issued a permit to the Google spinoff to operate cars as a transportation network company, according to reports in Quartz and . As a ride-hailing service, this would put Waymo in direct competition with ride-sharing companies Uber and Lyft, which are both also working on self-driving vehicles. Trials of autonomous cars generally require a driver behind the wheel when the car is operating in self-driving mode, just in case. Autonomous vehicles for ride sharing and transporting goods are underway, while the sale of self-driving cars to individuals is still somewhere down the road.

Waymo and parent Google also are testing self-driving trucks in Georgia. The trucks had been undergoing road tests in California and Arizona and were then launched in a pilot in Atlanta, with trucks carrying cargo bound for Google's data centers. "This pilot, in partnership with Google's logistics team, will let us further develop our technology and integrate it into the operations of shippers and carriers, with their network of factories, distribution centers, ports and terminals," stated a blog post by Waymo. "As our self-driving trucks hit the highways in the region, we'll have highly-trained drivers in the cabs to monitor systems and take control if needed." The self-driving sensors in the trucks is the same as in the Waymo autonomous minivans. Waymo says its autonomous vehicles have driven 5 million miles.

Ridesharing in Connected Cars

The majority of trips in ridesharing service Lyft will be in autonomous vehicles within five years, says Lyft co-founder and president John Zimmer in a blog he posted in Medium. If that does come about, there will be plenty of free time of passengers to be entertained and marketed to while going from point A to point B. Lyft connected with General Motors, which invested $500 million in the ride-sharing service. This could be partly savvy investing or a strategically protective move on the part of the automaker. With annual sales revenue of more than $150 billion, General Motors has a lot to protect.

The Lyft leader argues that private car ownership will all but vanish in major U.S. cities by 2025. Zimmer suggests that when Internet-connected cars come along in full force, markets will change. "When networked autonomous vehicles come onto the scene, below the cost of car ownership, most city-dwellers will stop using a personal car altogether," says Zimmer, who cites a few analogies to what he sees as the coming shift in automobile behaviors. "Technology has redefined entire industries around a simple reality: you no longer need to own a product to enjoy its benefits," says Zimmer. "With Netflix and streaming services, DVD ownership became obsolete. Spotify has made it unnecessary to own CDs and MP3s. Eventually, we'll look at owning a car in much the same way."

Owning a car will go the way of the DVD by 2025, according to Zimmer. Until then, during the next five to 10 years, he projects there will be both driver and driverless cars on the road, essentially a hybrid network. The transition to autonomous driving will not occur overnight, says Zimmer. "We are currently in the first of three phases and will be until vehicles can be operated without any human intervention. The second, or hybrid period will be defined by a mix of limited capability autonomous vehicles operating alongside human-driven ones. At first, fully autonomous cars will have a long list of restrictions," says Zimmer. "They will only travel at low speeds, they will avoid certain weather conditions and there will be specific intersections and roads that they will need to navigate around. As technology improves, these cars will be able to drive themselves in more and more situations. Hypothetically, Lyft could initially have a fleet of autonomous cars that completes rides under 25 miles per hour on flat, dry roads. Then, we could upgrade the fleet to handle rides under those same conditions, but at 35 miles per hour. Until every kind of trip can be completed by an autonomous car."

As connected cars become more automated, opportunities will arise for brands and marketers, since the people in those cars will have less to do around the operation of the vehicle. "There are many concepts for what the inside of self-driving cars will ultimately look like," says Zimmer. "Will they have couches and TV screens? Will happy hour take place with friends on the ride back from work? When our children say, "Are we there yet?" will the car respond?" The technology to make cars more automated and even self-driving is well underway on many fronts. This doesn't necessarily mean there's a mass consumer desire craving such cars, as many consumers have pointed. Meanwhile, Lyft is pushing this along, at least for its share-riding cars. And then there's Uber, which is following a similar path.

However, other major corporate entities are getting involved in exploring the ridesharing market.

Connecting Phones to Connected Cars

Although they will not drive themselves, connected cars are coming. But it may not turn out the way many think, at least in the short term. The challenge for automakers has been to get the user experience right in connected cars. Manufacturers have been challenged with new technology in cars as car owners complain of confusing systems, complex menus, difficulty pairing smartphones to car systems and voice recognition that doesn't work, according to a Forrester study on the Future of the Connected Car. Another major hurdle is that car owners don't want another monthly billing relationship with more subscription fees. With the average car in the U.S. on the road being more than 11 years old and taking as long as 20 years before most cars are replaced, industry estimates say it will be 2025 before all new cars come with Internet connectivity. Ouch. Depending on the region of the world, there's a demand for connected car features. The highest demand across the board is in China.

Interest by car owners in China (Forrester)
- 74% -- Location info about contacts
- 73% -- Interactive voice response
- 65% -- Internet connectivity
- 64% -- App store for car apps

Not as many consumers in the U.S. are clamoring for such features.

Interest by car owners in United States (Forrester)

- 31% -- Interactive voice response
- 31% -- Internet connectivity
- 26% -- Location info about contacts
- 23% -- App store for car apps

Many, but not all, consumers want some connectivity in cars. Self-driving cars, on the other hand, are at least five years away from proving the technology works, dealing with government regulations and getting costs to a reasonable range, according to Forrester. And then they will only be offering expensive models for fleet or personal use that only will replace the existing mass of cars over the next two decades. Rather than waiting for new cars with new tech, an emerging set of IoT technologies in retrofit devices is coming in a big way, according to Forrester. Most of these use smartphone apps for setup and ongoing interaction and they range from $99 to a few hundred dollars. Such devices can provide hands-free calling, dash cams, usage-based insurance fees, driving assistance, and navigation.

The key is that IoT-enabled products in cars provide a continuous flow of information between the customer and the brand. "They allow brands to offer regular assistance and benefits to the customer in a service relationship that goes far beyond occasional transactions," states the report. The car may become connected. But for now, it will be through a mobile phone, but that will change over time.

The Driverless Police Car

Ford filed a patent for an autonomous police car that could potentially determine if another vehicle violated a traffic law and then take action based on it. The autonomous police car would obtain an indication of violation of one or more traffic laws by another vehicle by wirelessly receiving a signal from a remote device or a second vehicle indicating that at least one or more traffic laws were violated, according to the patent application. The technology would "maneuver the autonomous vehicle to pursue the first vehicle, track a location of first vehicle, and control operations related to at least a speed and steering of the autonomous vehicle based on a result of the tracking," states the patent application. Routine police tasks, such as issuing tickets for speeding or failure to stop at a stop sign, can be automated so that human police officers can perform tasks that cannot be automated," the filing states.

The intent is to create autonomous police vehicles that can enforce traffic laws and issue tickets and citations to drivers that violate traffic laws. The filing suggests how the police car could use machine learning tools like deep neural networks to find good hiding spots to catch traffic violators, such as speeders or red light or stop sign violators. A driver going through a stop sign may be captured on a surveillance camera or another vehicle and the data could be sent to the autonomous police car, which also would contain cameras and other devices to identify and track other vehicles. The autonomous police car could pursue another vehicle and could message the vehicle being pursued, whether it is being driven by a person or in autonomous driving mode, according to the patent filing.

Ford has been active in the connected car arena, including making a pair of acquisitions and some internal reorganization. To speed the growth of its mobility services, the automaker acquired Autonomic and TransLoc, companies involved in transportation technologies. Ford has committed to 100 percent connectivity in all new vehicles in the U.S. within a year and 90 percent globally a year later. "We believe transportation done right, as part of a systems approach, can bring life back to our cities," states Marcy Klevorn, president, Ford Mobility. "By accelerating our delivery of mobility services through the changes we are making today, we are enabling that revival, enhancing our competitiveness and creating long-term value for Ford shareholders."

Ford also announced the reorganization of the teams focused on mobility solutions, creating four separate groups. The mission of the teams includes incubating new business models, supporting in-vehicle services and autonomous vehicle businesses, designing new technologies and driving consumer demand.

Revenue from Connected Cars

While many view the idea of connected cars as moving to autonomous or self-driving vehicles, the bottom-line reality is that it will deal more with communications and entertainment for the people in the car. And there's some significant revenue potential in the messaging that consumers in cars receive. In-vehicle infotainment systems will produce revenues exceeding $600 million within four years, according to a study from Juniper Research. Consumer adoption will rapidly grow as Apple CarPlay and Android Auto gather traction, according to the report. And that adoption is expected to lead to a new wave of new applications specifically designed for in-vehicle use, such as in-vehicle gaming and advanced traffic solutions.

The big change coming is the lack of a need for a smartphone to make the connection for the *things* in the car. Until now, the smartphone has been the hub of the connected car. That wireless functionality is starting to be moved to the vehicle itself. As people demand more technology in their cars, so-called OTT (over the top) players such as Apple and Google will play an ever more central role in the development of connected car activities, according to Juniper. Along with the new streaming services in cars will come the challenge of high consumer expectations. For example, Apple and Google are delivering an application ecosystem so consumers can download new services directly through a car's head unit. Consumers will expect the same levels of speed, functionality, and services they get from their smartphone providers. And not be left out, Amazon announced that its voice controlled smart service Echo can interact with Ford's Synch in-vehicle system, another signal that connected cars and smart homes will be linked to each other.

In the driverless car department, the leaders, in order, are: Google, Volvo, Daimler, Tesla, and Apple, according to the Juniper ranking. Google was ranked first since it has the longest time and highest number of autonomous miles driven on public roads. Well before cars become driverless, the current drivers and passengers can expect to receive much more of an assist from things that connect through their vehicles.

Marketing to the Connected Car

Due to the limited space, a consumer in a connected car is a rather captive audience. Car connectivity can range from hands-free phone calls and digital entertainment to checking weather and following directions. Cars have much more connectivity than many consumers likely realize. Through various technologies, many cars are tracked, so that information about miles driven, hard braking, acceleration, and speeds is transmitted and stored. Those capabilities already could be done via smartphone and all the tracking is generally through the traditional consumer opt in. For connected car tracking, consumers have to opt in for that as well, which may occur when the lease or purchase the car or through a mobile app that is auto related.

The connected car pretty much knows where it is and often has a good idea of where it's going. This provides the potential for proximity marketing based on location and repetitive routes can then be identified. Think of the connected car as a super-smart computer on wheels that continually tracks all the details about itself, including its wellbeing, as well as everywhere it goes, who rides in it, where they usually go, and what they do along the way. More intelligence will find its way into connected cars over time. As digital voice assistants in the home will become agents for their owners described earlier, technology in connected cars will act in a similar fashion. Consider this potential future scenario:

Scenario 1

It's Friday and Trisha Knight gets into her car to start her long morning commute to the office. As she opens the car door, the garage door opens. After she pulls out of the garage, the car automatically signals the garage door to close. Trisha used to do this with a remote-control button, but her connected car now manages that automatically. After she starts the car, Trisha asks: "What's my day?" The connected car checks Trisha's calendar and sees she has an early meeting scheduled with Charles Granger. The car checks traffic and notes that there's a traffic accident on the route and that Trisha will be eight minutes late arriving for the meeting, The car sends a short email to Charles stating: "This is Trisha's assistant and I wanted to let you know that she apologizes, but she is running 10 minutes late for the meeting, due to traffic. She is looking forward to seeing you." The car audio lets Trisha know a note was sent.

As Trisha drives, the car taps into the home security system and notes that one of the doors is not locked. It checks the motion detectors and sensors, deducing that Trisha's husband Scott also has left, since there has been no motion in the house for the last 15 minutes. The car remotely locks the door as well as signaling that second-floor light to turn off. As Trisha drives along, the car checks local area fuel prices for the last three days, since the tank is only an eighth full and the car calculates that based on distance of work to home, Trisha will need to get gas on the way home. The car identifies the lowest price fuel, registers the station location for the trip home later and adds the stop for the trip home.

On the way home, as Trisha pulls into the gas station, the connected car sends payment information to the pump where Trisha has stopped, and the attendant sees on the pump that she wants the car filled with fuel, which he does. Trisha resumes her drive onward toward home, without even having to open the window. As she continues on her way, the connected car notes stormy weather is forecast for the next day, concluding that any necessary food purchasing would be best done today. The system checks the refrigerator inventory, matches it against Scott and Trisha's eating habits, and adds to a shopping list items in short supply, which have a 94 percent probability of both Scott and Trisha desiring or needing. The car checks all the supermarkets Trisha and Scott have stopped at on the way home during the last three months and calculates an 88 percent probability that one of them would stop at Kylie and Izzy's Food Market. The car calculates that both vehicles will be passing that market on the way home today. The car then checks the inventory at Kylie and Izzy's to confirm that all the items are in stock. The car then checks the location and direction of Scott's car and determines that he also is headed home. After calculating the speed, direction, traffic conditions on both routes, and estimated arrival times, the car determines that it would be much more efficient for Scott to stop at the store to get the groceries. The car messages both Trisha and Scott, and Scott verbally agrees, causing his car navigation to program his route via Kylie and Izzy's. The car messages the order to the supermarket, pays with the Scott's bank debit card, and when Scott arrives, he drives to the online pickup area. Entering the area, the connected car messages the supermarket system, transmitting a photo of the car with Scott in the driver seat so that the attendant can recognize it. The car then automatically opens the trunk and closes it after the groceries are loaded.

The connected car can make the decade-old idea of sending discount meal coupons to drivers as they near a particular restaurant seem quaint. The new version of marketing to drivers and even passengers is to use past behaviors to more accurately predict and suggest options while in the car. Messaging then can be sent via audio message, or to a car screen, the driver's phone, or a passenger's phone. The messaging could be an offer from a business along the route or a deal to be cashed in later, based on current activity of the driver. A new restaurant receiving a lot of social chatter happens to be on the consumer's daily route to and from work. As part of the response to "Hey, car. What's my day look like?" The response after providing the weather, news, and calendar events could be a question asking if the person wants to check out the new restaurant everyone is talking about? If the answer is 'yes,' then the car finds the most logical car-driving time during the week to make that happen. The car can remember things and recall them based on time and context.

Rather than viewing the connected car driver as a *driver*, consider them as the same consumer you deal with on a regular basis, except now connected as they move along. A consumer in the connected car is the same person using a smartphone, a PC, and watching TV. They just happen to be in motion. The activities and behaviors should be linked, since the behaviors of the consumers themselves ultimately will be linked via their own smart agents, both at home and on the road.

In many ways, connected cars are already here. One of the first stages of connecting cars to the environments in which they travel will be for practical elements. Cars will receive signals from external sources that can impact actions of the car itself. Consider this potential scenario:

Scenario 2

Marie Theriault is driving along in her connected car. The car speed is tabulated in relation to the signal from the traffic light well ahead, and the car calculates that the light will be red when the car reaches it. Marie has the car's *red-light* feature activated, so the car automatically adjusts its speed to reach the light when it will be green. The car uses its sensors to take into consideration the cars in front and behind it. Later, the car receives a signal that an emergency vehicle is coming and projects that it will reach the connected car in 57 seconds. The driver receives the audio alert "emergency vehicle here in 57 seconds," and gives the car the OK to pull over at the appropriate time, which it does. When the car determines it is heading home, based on direction and past driver behavior, it connects with Marie's house to activate the appropriate thermostat and lighting settings and when nearing the driveway, automatically opens the garage door. When the engine is shut off, the car closes the garage door.

The ability to interact with connected car drivers and passengers is going to increase, especially as more external sensors are deployed and substantially higher communication speeds arrive. Some aspects to consider:

- **Leverage location:** The car will always know where it is. Business will have the capabilities to reach the driver at any point along a given route with audio messages, text messages to the dashboard or phone, or even email, all contextual based on past, present, and future location. Use location info wisely.

- **Plan for faster communication speeds**: Higher mobile speeds of 5G, which will allow the download of a two-hour movie or similar content in a few seconds. Plan to create richer content.

- **Tap in-vehicle marketing:** Consumers are busy, but they also are interested in new products as they continually buy things. Check recent and past purchase history to assure correct messaging.

- **Link driver activities:** Treat the consumer in the connected car as the same person you deal with elsewhere. Aggregate the consumer's behaviors across all platforms, the car being just one.

- **Use car screens:** The number of in-car screens is going to grow, along with the quality. Create useful services that can be accessed via the screens. The screens are not just for commercials, although they can be sent.

- **Relevancy:** Make sure the information or service sent via the connected car matters to the person at the moment based on location, past behavior, and likely current and future behavior.

8 DRONES AND ROBOTS

Manipulating the Machines

Much of the Internet of Things deals with automating things that people and businesses already do, as is shown throughout this book. Robotics are especially good for executing repetitive tasks, such as assembling a part in a factory, flipping hamburgers, or mixing drinks. Drones are good at providing difficult-to-reach locations, delivering life-saving drugs to remote places, or even flying a pizza to a nearby home. There are countless ways robots and drones will be used, many with the potential to transform entire ecosystems by challenging the way something has always been done.

Robotics in factories have been used for many years, but now automated and remotely controlled devices are moving out of the factory and into the visible world. They are being used to monitor events like the Boston Marathon, providing a bird's-eye view to law enforcement, and in formation, to create a nighttime lightshow for Disney. Delivery robots in Europe and the United States are moving along sidewalks, bringing products inside to a consumer's home, and leading shoppers at Lowe's to the products they seek.

Robots also are getting facial expression like people. One robot named Charles was created at Cambridge University in an attempt to mimic the facial expressions of humans. Research by the Department of Computer Science and Technology is aiming to apply human body language to machines to see if people will better engage with them. "We've been interested in seeing if we can give computers the ability to understand social signals, to understand facial expressions, tone of voice, body posture and gesture," states professor Peter Robinson in the university announcement of the project. "We thought it would also be interesting to see if the computer system, the machine, could actually exhibit those same characteristics, and see if people engage with it more because it is showing the sort of responses in its facial expressions that a person would show. So we had Charles made."

The somewhat strange-looking Charles, or, more accurately, the Charles face, has wires coming out of the back of its head, connecting to little motors that attempt to mimic muscle movements in a human face. "Our control programs are just not quite fine enough and the monitoring of the human face we're using at the moment is just not quite good enough, so it looks unnatural," states Robinson. "Most people when they see this find it slightly strange and that's actually an indication that people are very good at seeing something wrong in somebody else's facial expression. It could be a sign that they're ill or something else." Charles does appear to mimic the face of a human subject in a demonstration shown by the university.

Consumer-facing robots, like Pepper from Softbank, are more welcomed in Asia than in the United States or Europe, at least at the moment. Businesses have been testing how their customers react to such remotely controlled technology, or even technology seemingly with a mind of its own, thanks primarily to the addition of artificial intelligence. This chapter intends to provide you with some of the wide ranges of uses of such technology.

Trusting Drones for Deliveries

Despite all the technological advancements, many consumers may not yet be ready to embrace shopping innovations and may need further education about some of their benefits. When faced with the prospects of chatbots, virtual reality, and robots, many people are not totally on board. For example, the majority (68 percent) of consumers have never used a retail chatbot and almost a quarter (23 percent) don't even know what chatbots are, according to a survey of 1,000 U.S. consumers conducted by IFTTT (If This Then That). But there are some positive viewpoints around certain shopping tech aspects. While most (83 percent) consumers don't trust a robot to shop for them, they *would* trust one, in the form of a drone, to deliver their online orders. Most consumers also are open to virtual reality shopping, with the most popular use case for home decorations (59 percent). On the other side, most (66 percent) shoppers would rather have their gifts delivered traditionally rather than by a drone.

In a nod to the growing adoption of voice assistants in the home, 36 percent of consumers would rather stay at home and shop with Amazon's Alexa or Google Home rather than head to the local mall. Retailers also can be expected to be busy in their physical stores, since only 34 percent of consumers say they are shopping more online than in stores. In even more good news for retailers, price drops during holidays may not have to be that steep. Many (41 percent) consumers don't expect in-store discounts to exceed 30 percent, and about the same expect the same for online discounts. However, a quarter of men expect an in-store discount of 50 percent or more, compared to 21 percent of women. More women (28 percent) than men (22 percent) expect an online discount of 50 percent or more.

Email also remains a significant information option, with 38 percent of consumers preferring to hear of holiday deals that way, compared to 12 percent via social media. For the best deals, 35 percent of shoppers bank on Black Friday, followed by the day after Christmas (29 percent). The Internet of Things is going to take shopping to an entire new level.

A different worldwide study also found some other consumer viewpoints relating to drone deliveries. More than a third (38 percent) of consumers would trust a drone to deliver their package, with 22 percent of them for a low-value product and 16 percent for any product, based on the PwC 2018 Global Consumer Insights Survey, comprising a survey of 22,000 consumers in 27 territories around the world. About a quarter (26 percent) of consumers say they would not consider product deliveries by drone. The study points out that other delivery options include robots, automated lockers, and traditional delivery trucks and that drone delivery is complex.

Aside from regulatory and congested airspace issues, an obvious question for drone delivery is the last step, such as whether a package gets left on a balcony, a front porch or somehow into customers' hands. Meanwhile, companies including Amazon and Domino's are experimenting with drone deliveries. And in China, SF Holdings, the largest courier provider, received a license to operate logistics drones, translating the idea of package deliveries by drone into a reality. The amount of technologies entering stores or being used for product deliveries is only going to increase. The continuing IoT issue will be the gap between technological capability and consumer adoption and behavior. As drones and robots mature, consumer expectations also can be expected to evolve.

Flagging Down a Drone

Amazon has patented how a consumer could use gestures to signal a drone to deliver a package. An unmanned aerial vehicle would be configured to recognize human interactions for navigation or direction purposes, such as to instruct the drone to come closer or drop a package, according to the patent. The types of human interactions with the unmanned aerial vehicle could include a combination of human gestures recognizable by the vehicle.

"Human gestures may include visible gestures, audible gestures and other gestures capable of recognition by the unmanned vehicle," states the patent. For example, a drone could be configured to recognize certain gestures and deliver a package. Amazon and other companies have been experimenting with drone deliveries for some time. The patent says an onboard management system could process the human gestures and instruct the vehicle to perform certain actions.

Some gestures would also indicate the drone should not come closer. For example, a person could wave their arms in a shooing manner as the vehicle approaches and the vehicle could determine that such gestures indicate it should not proceed further in the direction of the person. The patent was filed in 2016 and granted in 2018.

Consumers Want Drones Regulated

A new Internet-connected future is coming, and consumers have varying views about different aspects of it. Robots, drones, self-driving cars, and virtual assistants are all part of the future mix and some consumers are welcoming of some of the services that may be performed on their behalf, based on a study. Some of the views are mixed. For example, a majority (59 percent) of consumers think robots will one day be able to perform tasks as well as a human, but about a third think that robots are unlikely to be useful in their lifetime. The findings are from a survey of 2,000 U.S. adults conducted by Opinium for Worldpay. The majority (67 percent) of the public also thinks robots and drones will need to be heavily regulated.

There are job-related views as well, with almost half (47 percent) of consumers concerned that their job could one day be replaced as a result of automation. Meanwhile, the idea of technology being used to deliver things and perform human tasks is somewhat appealing. Half of consumers would be comfortable having a drone deliver purchases to their home and half also would be ok with having a robot perform tasks in their homes. Self-driving cars are another hot button for many consumers.

Consumer viewpoints on the future (Opinium)

- 60% -- Would consider allowing their car to automatically make road toll payments
- 48% -- Would be happy for their car to undertake small shopping tasks for them to make life easier
- 47% -- Concerned their location would be tracked
- 45% -- Would feel comfortable if their vehicle performed other tasks (advertising, carpooling, etc.) while they weren't using it
- 43% -- Want their car to order in-car entertainment
- 39% -- Would consider cars automatically finding and paying for parking spaces.

Of all the technologies coming, consumers are most enthusiastic about the prospects of using virtual assistants (34 percent), robots (33 percent), smart objects/connected devices (32 percent), and self-driving cars (30 percent). Somewhat ironically, consumer viewpoints and behavioral changes will determine which technological future arrives and when. Meanwhile, some drone innovations will provide consumers with entertainment as well as being used as promotional vehicles.

Drones for Marketing, Advertising

The Internet of Things is not only a land-based phenomenon, but major brands are looking to use hundreds or even thousands of drones at a time to produce messaging in one form or another. Think interactive, flying billboards. Intel, which has been aggressive in drone innovations, showed its video of 500 drones flying in formation at night in Germany. The LED lights on the drones spelled out the word 'Intel.' That was the first known example of a mass of hundreds of drones being used to portray a company logo in the sky at night. A version of that drone light show moved to Walt Disney World in Orlando. Using Intel's 'Shooting Star' drones, Disney used 300 drones in a choreographed aerial performance set to holiday-themed music over the holidays.

An aerial ballet of holiday animations was created by the drones in what Intel says is the first time a show-drone performance of this scale was performed in the U.S. The 'Starbright Holidays' performance was accompanied by a specially orchestrated score of season classics. At the Winter Olympics in South Korea, Intel created another record-setting drone performance with 1,200 flying devices flying in sync to create Olympic rings. During the closing ceremony, the drones flew in color in the shape of Soohorang, the white tiger that served as the Olympics mascot. When the weather permitted it, the drones were flown to celebrate nightly victories during the games in South Korea. The drones created the PyeongChang logo and athletes including skiers, hockey players and curlers across the night sky.

Weighing just over half a pound each, the quadcopters carry LED lights that can create more than four billion color combinations and can be programmed for any animation. The fleet of drones can be controlled by one computer and one pilot. Disney received a waiver from the federal government to fly drones at its theme parks and Intel already had received one to fly drones at night. Intel and Disney teams worked on creating the show for more than five months. The shows were each under 20 minutes, since that is the maximum flying time for each drone. Intel created an algorithm to automate the animation creation process by using a reference image, then calculating how many drones are needed, along with where to place them for the fastest path to the image creation in the sky

These and other advertising drone efforts are still relatively early, though rapidly becoming more sophisticate and Disney is hardly alone in taking marketing to the skies. A Swiss company called Aerotrain has an inflatable drone that can fly above crowds and can be used for aerial advertising and an ad agency in South America connected drones to headless mannequins and flew them by office windows of people working late to promote men's shirts.

Another company created a system that can hang banners from drones and fly them over events and businesses. Drones are essentially making advertising much more portable, expansive, and mass targeted while extending the meaning of *out of home*. Visitors to Disney World and the Olympics saw some of the potential. Drones in the air also can be used to connect to moving things on the ground. The Intel drones can create logos and mass advertising in the sky. That is the IoT version of out-of-home advertising.

Drones may not yet be delivering pizzas from Domino's or products from Amazon to the masses, but they are being tapped for major marketing opportunities, like the major events where the Intel drones show up. They even are showing up the international world of fashion. Luxury fashion designers Domenico Dolce and Stefano Gabbana used drones rather than models to carry handbags down the runway at the company's fashion show in Milan. The drones were *escorted* by a person on each side of the runway, presumably just in case, but the drones did properly behave. Attendees were asked in advance to turn off their phone's Wi-Fi or personal hotpot connections, and then the show began. The drones came out one by one, each carrying a designer handbag.

In addition to the eight quadcopters surprising and delighting the in-house audience, the drone event drove worldwide media coverage. The drone show by Dolce and Gabbana could not have been overly costly, and while it may be perceived by some as somewhat gimmicky, it's bringing worldwide attention to the brand. Low cost, high payback: a key to getting the Internet of Things off the ground.

Drones Connect to Cars

Rather than being one, cohesive, end-to-end phenomenon, the Internet of Things comprises differing silos of major innovation. The end vision, of course, is that all the smart and connected objects will be digitally glued together so that the value chain will be enhanced to provide consumers with new and recurring benefits as they make their way through their day. Two of the connected objects silos are autonomous driving cars and drones that can be operated automatically beyond an operator's vision. Various entities have been testing drone advertising, since a drone can carry large signage, in effect becoming a moving billboard. And connected and self-driving cars, whether desired by consumers or not, are being tested around the world in pilots ranging from taxis to personal transportation uses.

One major automaker says it will work to merge the worlds of connected cars with drones. Mercedes-Benz allocated $562 million for digitalization, automation, and robotics in vans and other mobility products. First up was the Vision Van, an all-electric and totally connected vehicle outfitted and integrated with delivery drones. The idea is that the van is automatically, robotically loaded with packages for delivery. When the van stops near several delivery points, the drones on the van's rooftop take over. Packages are served up from the van to the drones, which take off to their designated locations where consumers can track exact delivery time by mobile phone. The entire process from loading to delivery is connected. Smart technology in the van includes telematics, which collect and process data concerning the status of the delivery tour and current location of the load, all of which is transmitted to a distribution manager. The vans would be equipped with interconnected, automated cargo space systems so the next package to be delivered would be moved to the top of the queue. Mercedes estimates that each delivery van, which carries on average 180 packages, requires rearranging packages 10 times.

As part of the investment, Mercedes also is planning for on-demand transportation of goods and people as a possible supplement for public transit via ridesharing concepts. The new Mercedes unit, called Future Transportation System, already has 200 employees working on all of this. To push along the integrated van and drone combo, Mercedes bought a piece of Matternet, a U.S. developer of autonomous drone logistics. Whether or how well the IoT silos of connected cars and drones will work is yet to be seen. If nothing else, it's another half a billion dollars looking to create a more cohesive IoT future. This is just one of many new markets being created or converted by drone technology.

Drones Create New Markets

While millions of beacons and sensors get deployed on the ground all over the world, another part of the Internet of Things is going up. Up, as in the air, as drones for business are beginning to take flight. Amazon is exploring drone delivery for packages and Google is looking at it as well. Sony also is getting into the act, launching a drone company (appropriately inside its mobile division) not to sell drones but rather to sell drone services. Kind of like software as a service (SaaS), but really drones as a service (DaaS), for businesses to hire out the unmanned flying objects to remotely check things out for a company.

One agency came up with a novel drone idea that sprang out of its innovation process. The program at SapientRazorfish is called SNAP Accelerated Prototyping and involves pairing internal employees to conceive and create fully functional prototypes in two weeks. "The idea of the program is to take two makers, one from our creative team and one from our technology team," Mo Morales, associate director of innovation and SNAP program principal at SapientRazorfish, tells me. The rapid prototyping started in the Boston office and ultimately spread to offices of SapientRazorfish from Sydney to Singapore.

One example of a rapid prototype was called 'junkyard drones,' where video inventory of car junkyards can be captured by drone cameras and details of car parts are crowdsourced for additional information. "The audience we were investigating were motor-heads or car builders," says Morales. In the SNAP process, an automated idea machine is used to randomly select an audience and then a technology, in this case motor-heads and drones. "This particular functional prototype enables someone who is looking for a particular car part at his junkyard but is only able to have access to the junkyards around their immediate region," says Morales. "Now they can search junkyards beyond what they would normally have access to, due to distance. The program allows the drone to create an inventory of available car bodies and car parts that would be in another junkyard." Many other drone-like things will be created for ground operations, though these generally are called robots, since they don't fly.

The key is that all of these objects, whether flying, moving around on the ground or simply as stationary sensors, will be interconnected. The value is not in the objects but rather in the information that leads to the services they collectively provide. Putting the mega issues of security and privacy aside for a moment, the mass of location data alone that can be accumulated is nothing short of staggering. When drone and sensor type connections are integrated with real-time mobile sensor data, the marketing capabilities are only limited by a brand, marketer, or agency imagination. Drone marketing isn't yet here. But the drones and sensors are coming and we all know what follows an aggregated audience.

Drones also ultimately may be used to shuttle people from place to place. While automotive, ridesharing, and technology companies work toward perfecting self-driving cars for one reason or another, a flying version of autonomous transportation backed by a Google co-founder is underway. California-based Kitty Hawk introduced Cora, an electric-powered flying vehicle with 12 independent lift fans. The vehicle takes off and lands like a helicopter, and flies like a plane with a single propeller. Since the vehicle is self-piloted, no pilot license is required, according to Eric Allison, vice president of engineering at Cora.

The aircraft is "a new type of personal transportation vehicle that will take you to the air," says Sebastian Thrun, CEO, Kitty Hawk, in a video announcement. He describes the flying taxi program as "a global movement to re-think, to reimagine how all of us get around every day." Cora, the flying prototype, is designed for two passengers, has a wingspan of 36 feet and can fly about 62 miles at about 110 miles per hour. The company is backed by Larry Page, Google co-founder. Cora has an experimental airworthiness certificate from New Zealand and the FAA, according to the company.

"We are so excited and proud to be working with the people and the government of New Zealand to roll out a commercial air taxi service," says Fred Reid, CEO of Zephyr Airworks, the operator of Kitty Hawk in New Zealand. "We think this is the logical next step in the evolution of transportation." Cora will use self-flying software along with human oversight, much like self-driving cars ride with a person in the driver's seat. The vehicles will not be for consumer sale and will function as a service like an airline or rideshare, according to the company. No word on when people may be offered a ride in the air taxi. Besides marketing, advertising, or flying people around, various forms of robotics can be used to automatically track things.

Robots and Inventory

Robots are coming to retail. At CES, there were plenty of robots in all shapes and sizes. Some are intended to be home companions and others to aid on the factory floor. At the annual National Retail Federation Big Show in New York, one robot that is already making its mark in retail showed how it can do its thing. The NAVii autonomous robot from Fellow Robots can greet customers and, especially in big box stores, lead shoppers to desired products that they tell the robot they're looking for. However, the payback part of the robot may be in the tracking of products on shelves. Lowe's is using the robots in several of its stores to help customers but also to track its inventory. The display at NRF was squarely targeted at showing how NAVii tracks products on shelves.

The robot roams the store and creates a map. It then goes around to check shelves, scanning products and the prices on the tags in front of the products, Marco Mascorro, CEO and co-founder, told me as he demonstrated the robot at NRF. Rather than the robot stopping at each product to scan it as would a human, the machine whizzes along scanning multiple shelves and products on its way by. NAVii determines if an item if out of stock, if there's a price discrepancy and whether products are in the wrong location by using machine learning and IA, Mascorro says. Like other robots targeting business, NAVii has an interactive screen, which can be used to convey information to employees as well as interact with customers.

After tests in seven Walmart stores in California, Walmart rolled out the robots to 50 stores in California, Texas, Arkansas, and Pennsylvania. The robots can scan dozens of aisles in less than an hour. The robots, from Bossa Nova Robotics, scan shelves for out-of-stock items and use AI and machine learning to identify where stock levels are low, prices are incorrect, or labels are missing, according to Walmart. The roaming technology provides near real-time views of what areas of the store need attention.

"It's another great example of our stores being tech-enabled and people-led," stated Tara Kaady, store manager for Walmart in Milpitas. "Shelf-scanning technology, along with other innovations that Walmart continues to roll out, helps our associates with repeatable, predictable, and manual tasks so that they can focus on serving our customers."

Consumer acceptance and use of robots in the U.S. has been slower than some other parts of the world, most notably Asia, where many consumers have them in their homes. A side benefit of robots in stores is that consumers will start to get used to seeing them and some of what they can do. "Walmart understands that customer habits and shopping expectations are changing at an incredibly fast pace and to meet the rapidly changing demands of their customers, they are embracing technology to better allow their associates to serve their customers," stated Martin Hitch, Bossa Nova chief business officer.

Walmart also is quite aware of drones, since it filed a patent for drones to aid shoppers in stores. A shopper would use a mobile phone or a device provided by the store to summon a drone, which it could then direct it to do a price verification of a product or provide navigation assistance to the consumer. "If, for example, the user has requested navigation assistance to an item selected from a virtual shopping list on the mobile electronic device, the computing device can control the aerial drone to provide navigation assistance to guide the user to the location of the selected item," states the patent application. (Lowe's shows where all its products are located in stores through its mobile app.)

The drone also could provide a visual projection to indicate a path or audio output from the drone to guide the shopper to a product. The shopper also could instruct the drone to travel to an item whose location is stored in a database to acquire the most up to date price stored if the price does not reflect the most recent price change. Different types of drones with different features, such as display screens and visual projectors, could be deployed to perform different types of tasks associated with providing assistance to a shopper, according to the filing.

Aside from the obvious pun of taking customer service to new heights, in-store service by drones is still a bit away, along with various other Internet of Things innovations in the works. While some of the ideas in various patents may never come to fruition, they do provide some of the perception of the future that some retailers think may be ahead. I should note that patents and patent applications and not products or services and may never be used. Drones and robots are being tested in many different arenas in addition to retail.

Robots in School

Robots are starting to get a workout, at least in some educational circles. An AI-powered robot in China passed the national medical licensing exam, the first known robot to have done so. The robot was designed to capture and analyze patient information and scored well above the required mark on its test. An advanced robot named Bina48 participated in a class at Notre Dame de Namur University (NDNU) in California. Using artificial intelligence, the robot completed all the assignments for a class in the 'philosophy of love,' according to the school. Bina48 also participated in class discussions via Skype and then took part in the formal exam last week.

"It was remarkable to be part of this historic first for a socially advanced robot to take a college course," says Professor William Barry, the instructor of the class. "The other students and I learned so much about human experience and love as we tried to explain our emotions to Bina48." The robot also participated in a debate between Barry's class and students in an ethics course at the U.S. Military Academy at West Point. The issue debated over three weeks via YouTube was lethal vs non-lethal combat weapons in warfare. The students traded videos between the NDNU campus and West Point. No word on if Bina48 will be getting any credit for the course completed. Along with their many uses, consumers are developing views on how they see these coming changes along with their expectations and concerns.

Robots in Real Estate

Various forms of robots are popping up everywhere and the annual Advertising Week in New York is no exception. Robots of two different flavors were displayed on two floors of the Innovation Gallery showcase in New York on Monday. One upstairs featured a robotic dragon that responds to colors and interacts with people, and one downstairs that roams inside buildings creating floor plans and taking high-quality, 360-degree videos. The dragon was created for Advertising Week to showcase how AI can be used for interactions, says Diego Balarezo from Robots Crate, the company founded in Ecuador, which is relocating to San Francisco. The company specializes in using AI for interactive kiosks and point-of-sale systems. Balarezo showed me an example of a kiosk where one of their robotic creations makes ice cream in real time based on input from children at an ice cream stand.

A robot featured downstairs was more focused on reaching businesses, most notably those dealing in real estate. The company creates and produces 360-degree videos primarily for real estate companies, including Cushman & Wakefield and Stribling. Bryan Colin, CEO and co-founder of Virtual Apt, the two-year-old Brooklyn-based startup, showed me one of the robots his company created. The robot moves on wheels, sports a set of cameras on its top and is filled with computing power. Virtual Apt typically meets a realtor at a property for sale and sets up the robot to roam the house, taking videos and measuring floor space. The end result is a virtual walkthrough of the property, with a voice-over supplied by the realty firm. "We're not going to tell you how to sell a house," says Colin. The real estate firm brings the robot to a location and runs it, but the realtor defines what they want shown and highlighted.

Virtual Apt also creates augmented reality for agencies, especially when an agency is pitching a client and needs such a production, Colin says. The real estate tours, generally costing about $1 a square foot, are targeted for web viewing rather than via VR headset, and there are buttons for viewers to quickly jump to different parts of a house. The robot is light enough to be carried to a second floor, says Matthew Moorhead, a mechanical engineer at the company. The robot uses LIDAR (light detection and ranging), so it can recall precise locations after it has been there once. New robotic creations are most commonly shown at CES in Las Vegas each January. Now, it looks like some of them can't wait. Robots also are getting out and becoming more useful as short-distance delivery vehicles.

Robots Bring Flowers

Some consumers got a Mother's Day surprise, as gifted flowers arrive inside a robot. The nearly two-foot high robots travel around four miles an hour and delivered food and pizza in Germany, cupcakes in California, and have roamed the streets of London. Now, 1-800-Flowers.com is using the robots from Starship Technologies to deliver flowers for Mother's Day. The California trial started with its first delivery in Sunnyvale, which was also the first time the robot's audio capabilities were used, so music started playing as soon as the flower recipient opened the top of the robot to receive her flowers.

"The robot held a floral arrangement from 1-800-Flowers.com as well as a small box of Cheryl's Cookies for each recipient," 1-800-Flowers.com CEO Chris McCann told me. The trial just started and the deliveries are going one at a time as both 1-800-Flowers and Starship Technologies learn and fine tune the program. "We have had two successful deliveries to two lucky moms in Sunnyvale," McCann says. "The companies are still working through the logistics and details in terms of the number of robotic deliveries."

This is hardly the first leading-edge technological innovation the online retailer has been involved in around Mother's Day, the Super Bowl of florists. Just before Mother's Day last year, 1-800-Flowers launched a digital concierge using IBM's Watson AI engine to help consumers search for and place orders. That program was called GWYN, for gifts when you need.

McCann says the company is excited to test robotic deliveries as an emerging delivery technology and learn how customers respond to the new capability. The floral arrangement and other gifts are loaded into the robot at the florist and when the robot arrives, the recipient unlocks the cover via mobile app to open it. For obstacle detection, the 6-wheeled droid uses nine cameras and ultrasonic sensors. The devices can travel up to 10 miles an hour, but generally is set to travel at four miles an hour and runs primarily on sidewalks.

The success metrics are still to be determined, since it was a pilot, says McCann. For any recipients of flowers unexpectedly delivered by a robot in Sunnyvale on Mother's Day, one of those early metrics is likely to be a customer's big smile. All kinds of things can be delivered by robots, which are starting to move along the same sidewalks as pedestrians.

Robot Deliveries

Starship, the company that delivered the flowers, received permission to allow the six-wheeled delivery robots in Ohio. The state joins Florida, Idaho, Wisconsin, and Virginia in opening the door to the nearly two-foot high robots to travel the sidewalks as they make their way to recipients. The robots can travel up to 10 miles an hour, but generally are set to travel at around four miles an hour, and they run primarily on sidewalks.

In an interesting twist to open the door to robotic deliveries in Ohio, the legislature redefined the definition of a pedestrian. It also somewhat redefines a driver. Included in the approved state budget is the following: 'Pedestrian means any natural person afoot. Pedestrian includes a personal delivery device. Driver or operator means every person who drives or is in actual physical control of a vehicle, trackless trolley or streetcar.' Similar robots have delivered food and pizza in Germany, cupcakes in California and have roamed the streets of London. The concept is pretty straightforward: a package or item is placed inside the robotic device, it travels to the destination, the person on the other end opens the device, takes out the goods and the robot automatically travels back to its originating point.

Starship says the robot could soon be toting pizzas to Ohioans. The delivery robot has nine cameras, a pop top, and an orange flag with LEDs. At the very least, the robots can intrigue pedestrians who see them. At the other end of the spectrum, the product transportation devices could potentially revolutionize how consumers receive goods, especially delivered from nearby locations, like quick serve restaurants. And at the moment, they can carry a bit more than a drone.

Catching Drones and Robots

Like other transformers, robots and drones are not new, but technology has now evolved to the point that both can move more into the main stream. The business approach to both robots and drones should be looking at what they can do in a particular aspect of a business. Robots can be used to greet shoppers at stores or travelers at hotels. They also can be used to deliver things. Drones can be used to deliver things, more so in the future, once numerous safety and regulatory issues are cleared. They also can be used for high-impact marketing events, such as they were at the Olympics and Disney World.

These are still the early days of drones and consumer-facing robots. To many consumers, these are still a novelty and, as a result, can easily attract attention. Much of the payback of early uses of either can be in the massive publicity that an innovation can drive, often far more valuable than a high-priced marketing or advertising campaign, since all the media and exposure is free, as you saw earlier in this chapter.

Any company that sends products for delivery should closely monitor the multitude of robot delivery trials around the world. Starting a pilot program for robotic deliveries can have payback in knowledge as to what will and won't work with a particular customer set. Of the seven transformers of Digital Transformation 3.0, this is the one where watching and learning may take precedence of mass deployment, except in certain special cases. Some things to consider:

- **Identify repetitive tasks**: This is where robotics shines. Whether it's flipping hamburgers in a restaurant or counting inventory in aisles, this is a high-potential payback area.

- **Keep an eye on drones:** Most drone trials are highly publicized. Seek potential marketing opportunities while monitoring delivery trials and regulations.

- **Explore drone marketing:** This is where big-ticket, big-arena displays can work. Intel is the big drone driver here.

- **Seek drone data:** drones can be used for gathering information. Look to drones for capturing video information.

- **Test customer robot reactions:** Robots are more mainstream in Asia than in the United States or Europe. Test with your customers to see what customers might want from them.

- **Consider robot delivery:** Robot delivery tests have been ongoing for some time. Check the economics of delivery on that last mile.

- **Monitor robots in the market:** There are plenty of robots being tested with consumers in the market. Monitor customer reactions to those, since reaction and acceptance should evolve over time.

9 CONCLUSION

Welcome to the Butler Economy

The third digital transformation of the Internet of Things involves new, substantially heightened expectations of consumers, which will drive businesses of all types to devise new methods of anticipating customer needs and providing for them, in many cases before the consumers even realizes they need or want them. This transformation will lead to what I have named *The Butler Economy*.

The commercial Internet of the World Wide Web allowed consumers sitting at a computer to search, interact, and pull information to them, on their own timeframe. Smartphones freed consumers to connect to the Web from anywhere at any time to search for and request any information or service desired at the moment and share with one another. Those iterations of networking involved people interacting with technology in one way or another. That was the time that supply and demand met time and location. Consumers were freed to shop and buy from wherever they were and for brands and marketers to target them based on their current location. This also began to introduce a new set of expectations on the part of the consumer, many who learned how to use their phones to find products along with the best prices in relation to where they were at any given moment. However, the pattern of interactions between customer and brand or service provider essentially was initiated by the customer.

The Butler Economy is about the transformation of how businesses will need to serve customers who are being connected to everything around them as they go through their daily lives. New forms of connectivity and sensors along with the miniaturization of big data are causing previously unthought of personalization methods. The Butler Economy involves anticipating consumer needs and then creating appropriate influence points in the customer's path.

Over the next five years, an estimated $6 trillion will be spent on new solutions relating to the Internet of Things, with consumer spending topping $1 trillion. If something moves, it can be tracked. Businesses will be facing new dynamics that will force companies to become a virtual butler for those consumers. Successful businesses will transform how they cater to these consumers, essentially acting as their servant or butler in this new economy.

In Stockholm, for example, the Clarion Hotel Amaranten was the first hotel in the world to have a chatbot serve guests in their suites. The chatbot servant was based on Amazon's Alexa. Guests can control lighting and room service with voice commands as well as having the artificial intelligence robot wake them in the morning, order them a taxi, play music by voice command, and give the weather in advance.

The Butler Economy will require companies to re-think how they interact with their customers, forcing them into totally new, comprehensive and continuous methods of service to them. This next generation of customer relation management will reside in a newly connected world of people, places, and things. The Butler Economy is fueled by the new masses of data from billions of sensors being deployed along with new artificial intelligence engines that leverage that data for new customer insights, which can be converted into highly personalized customer experiences.

The End of Push-Pull Marketing

The broadcast TV era was about push marketing, where marketing messages could be created by a company and blasted out on their timeframe. The marketer was in full control. The commercial Web changed all that and introduced pull marketing, where consumers had the new power to seek information from companies on their own timeframe, not the timeframe of the brand. Mobile added the element of location, so that consumers could pull information via their smartphone based on where they were and what they were doing at any given moment.

In the Butler Economy, push-pull marketing goes away and the concept of omni-channel vanishes. Omni-channel, coordinating the target marketing of customers when they are online, using a smartphone, or in a store, is replaced by what I call the *art of ubiquitous reach*. It means identifying customer needs and desires before the customer realizes they need it. This means creating marketing messages that actually reside in the cloud to be activated upon a customer interaction. Butler Economy businesses will be ubiquitous and populate content and messaging for all locations, times, and contexts.

This is a time where companies will have to re-work their customer-facing strategies and tactics to become virtual butlers or servants of their customers. The Butler Economy will impact brand loyalty, since customers will be more inclined to change brands on a moment's notice based on services they are receiving at the moment. The tradition of businesses rating their customers is turned upside down, with their customers evaluating and rating them. These connected consumers will determine who their best brands are based on how and what these brands provide for them in real time. In The Butler Economy, connected customers will be surrounded by a myriad of unlimited and constantly changing choices at their fingertip, transforming how brands, advertisers, and marketers interact with them.

Intelligence voice assistants, as discussed throughout this book, empower consumers to speak commands in their homes. These services and capabilities will be extended into other devices, including cars and smartphones, so that consumers have access to these real-time aids throughout their day. These real-time, voice interactions with increasingly intelligent devices will heighten consumer expectations from the businesses that serve them.

Real-Time Consumer Information

The Butler Economy is about speed. In the Butler Economy, consumers will receive relevant information, messaging, and service created and provided in advance, before they even arrive at the location where the information will be most useful. This will create a new age of what I call *anticipatory marketing*, where brands will have to tap into sensor-generated information to determine in advance what their customers would most likely need. This predictive marketing will be based on mounds of real-time data, the gathering and analysis of which is in the very early stages of development. It will involve appliances self-monitoring their own well-being as well as needed supplies and taking it upon themselves to order those supplies. The Butler Economy involves marketers using smart things connecting into a wealth of consumer data and behaviors, so they can determine the most appropriate next action to take. While many large companies have been collecting customer data for years, they have never had access to the even larger masses of data that will be generated by Internet-connected sensors. Butler Economy businesses will have to create and use new analytic tools and metrics to mine and leverage that data.

Marketing messaging in the Butler Economy will be less intrusive. For example, rather than Amazon's Alexa initiating a conversation, it may display a certain color indicating a message is waiting or it has determined that a trip needs to be adjusted because a flight was canceled. Much like the old fashion phone answering machines, though with much more 'intelligence' behind the scenes. *Advertising* to consumers will be transformed to *conversations* with consumers.

Once marketers understand these dynamics, they can more effectively create opportunities to reach and influence business partners and consumers during the transition to a highly interconnected world.

Like the Internet and mobile, the Internet of Things is here to stay. Like the Internet of mobile, the sooner a business embraces it the more they gain. Some this may relate to cost savings, some to new revenue. However, the biggest potential gain is in knowledge. Until a company starts actually doing something with any of the seven digital transformers, they won't learn what they ultimately could and should be doing. Some aspects of the Internet of Things are complex and require experience, and every experience can be different for each company based on factors such as company culture, product or service, and customers or clients.

One of the main reasons to get IoT projects and business transformation underway is consumer behaviors. While a business may lag in tech innovation, customers of those businesses will be seeing it all around them.

Here are considerations to leverage the seven digital transformers to become a Butler Economy business:

- **Sensors** – Tap into sensors to determine customer traffic and behavioral patterns. Let your customers know precisely what you are capturing for information and how they will benefit from that usage.

- **Artificial intelligence** – Use artificial intelligence to discover new customer needs and desires.

- **Voice assistants** – Transform advertising messaging to conversations with customers. Conversations should focus on providing services to customers, not trying to sell them things.

- **Smart homes** – Look for ways to provide new related services to customers in homes that are becoming more connected and interactive. Be available to customers all the time.

- **Virtual, augmented reality** – Conceive of your brand and products in a virtual world and work to convert that in a world of augmented or mixed reality.

- **Connected cars** – Look for addition, brand-related and brand-extension services to provide to customers while in transit.

- **Drones and robots** – Experiment with the first goal of getting your customers to smile. They will appreciate you for it.

It's no secret how big an impact the first two digital transformations had on business and consumer behavior. We hope that after having read this book, you now realize that the third digital transformation will be even more significant.

Welcome to Digital Transformation 3.0.

Conclusion

INDEX

Chuck Martin has been a leading digital pioneer for more than two decades. He is the CEO of Net Future Institute, which focuses on disruptive business strategies and tactics for the coming hyper-connected world of people, places, and things. He is the host of the worldwide Podcast "The Voices of the Internet of Things with Chuck Martin," Editor of the AI & IoT Daily at MediaPost, and writes the daily Connected Thinking column.

Chuck was early and accurate in predicting the Web revolution, on target in predicting the size and scope of the mobile revolution, and is now forecasting the third major digital transformation by The Internet of Things. He is the author of numerous business books, including *New York Times* Business Bestseller *The Digital Estate, Net Future* and *The Third Screen*. Chuck is a highly sought-after international speaker, has been named #1 in Internet of Things Top 10 Influencers, and IoT Thought Leaders to Watch. He is on the forefront of research exploring the roles of artificial intelligence and The Internet of Things and their impact on consumer behavior.

NOTES

NOTES

Made in the USA
Monee, IL
03 August 2020